MW01033794

Cessna 152
A Pilot's Guide

Jeremy M. Pratt

Aviation Supplies & Academics, Inc.
Newcastle, Washington

U.S. Edition 1995

© 1995 Aviation Supplies & Academics, Inc.

First published in England by Airplan Flight Equipment, Ltd.
and Jeremy M. Pratt, 1993

Cessna 152: A Pilot's Guide
Jeremy M. Pratt

ASA-PG-C-152
ISBN 1-56027-212-0

Aviation Supplies & Academics, Inc.
Newcastle, Washington

Printed in the United States of America

05 04 03 02   9 8 7 6 5 4 3

Pratt, Jeremy M.
     Cessna 152 / Jeremy M. Pratt. — U.S. ed.
         p.   cm. — (A pilot's guide.)
     Includes index.
     ISBN 1-56027-212-0
     1. Cessna 152 (Private planes) 2. Private flying. I. Title.
     II. Series: Pratt, Jeremy M. Pilot's guide.
     TL686.C4P732 1995
     629.132'5217—dc20   95-16302
                                 CIP

Acknowledgements

I would like to thank all those whose knowledge, help and advice went into this book; in particular:

Farooq Ahmed
CAA Safety Promotion Section
Colourmatch
Cheshire Air Training School
Deltair
Adrian Dickinson
Steve Dickinson
George Firbank
East Midlands Flying School
Peggy Follis
David Hockings
Andy Holland

Light Planes (Lancs) Ltd.
Luton Flight Training
Manchester School of Flying
Steve Maffitt
Chris Nolan
Andy Parker
Ravenair
Neil Rigby
Ian Sixsmith
John Thorpe
Visual Eyes

Sarah, Kate and Miles

Jeremy M. Pratt
June 1993

Contents

Section 3 – Handling the Cessna 152

Section 4 – Mixture and Carburetor Icing Supplement

Section 5 – Expanded Cessna 152 Pre-Flight Check List

Section 6 – Cessna 152 Loading and Performance

Section 7 – Conversions

Index

Editor's Note

Welcome to ASA's *A Pilot's Guide* series by Jeremy Pratt. In this guide, you'll learn from the experts the general principles involved in flying the Cessna 152, with extra insight on individual characteristics gleaned from flying experience.

Cessna 152: A Pilot's Guide is not an authoritative document. Material in this book is presented for the purposes of orientation, familiarization, and comparison only.

Performance figures are based upon the indicated weights, standard atmospheric conditions, level hard-surface dry runways, and no wind. They are values based upon calculations derived from flight tests conducted by the aircraft company under carefully documented conditions and using professional test pilots. Performance will vary with individual aircraft and numerous other factors affecting flight.

The approved *Pilot's Operating Handbook* and/or the approved *Airplane Flight Manual* is the only source of authoritative information for any individual aircraft. In the interests of safety and good airmanship, the pilot should be familiar with these documents.

Section 1
General Description

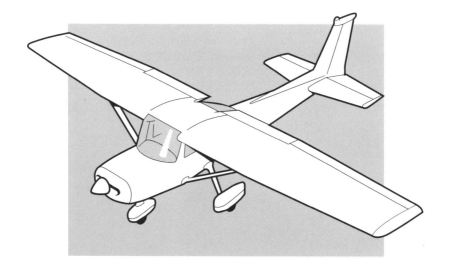

Introduction to the Cessna 152

At a glance, the Cessna 152 appears almost identical to the later model of the long-running Cessna 150 that it replaced; however, on closer inspection there are many differences.

The Cessna 152 was first introduced in 1977, after over 23,000 C150s had been produced. The Cessna 152 has a Lycoming 0-235-L2C engine, giving 110 HP, as opposed to the 100 HP Continental engine of the Cessna 150. The electrical system and fuel system are redesigned and the gross weight increased by 70 lbs. An Aerobat version was also produced (A152); in this version the airframe is "beefed up" to withstand the increased positive and negative loads involved in aerobatics.

As with its predecessor, the 152 was mostly built in Wichita, Kansas; although a significant number were built by Reims Aviation in France. The French built aircraft are identical to the USA built examples, but Reims aircraft model numbers are preceded with an "F"; i.e., F152 and FA152.

Through the production of the 152 there were few major design changes. In 1983 the Lycoming 0-235 N2C engine became standard. This engine featured a redesigned combustion chamber to overcome lead fouling problems experienced with the L2C. The spark plugs of the newer N2C engine apparently have a life up to three times that of the L2C. The horsepower is reduced slightly to 108 HP, speed and range are similarly affected. In 1984 the landing and taxi lights were moved from the lower cowling to the leading edge of the left wing.

Production of the 152 ceased in 1985 after over 7,000 aircraft had been built. It had become yet another victim of the vicious spiral of rapidly escalating production costs—caused not least by the USA's product liability situation—and falling demand. Many of the Cessna 150s built in the 1960s continue in daily flight school use, and there is no reason to believe that the Cessna 152 will not display the same longevity.

This publication deals with the standard 152, although much of the information is also relevant to the "Aerobat" models. As always the air-plane flight manual for the particular aircraft you are going to fly is the authoritative document.

PRODUCTION YEAR	MODEL	MODEL NAME
1978 – 1985	152	152/152II
1978 – 1985	F152	Reims/Cessna F152
		Reims/Cessna F152II

PRODUCTION YEAR	MODEL	MODEL NAME
1978 – 1985	A152	152 Aerobat
1879 – 1983	FA152	Reims/Cessna F152 Aerobat

The Airframe

The Cessna 152 airframe can be described as being of all metal construction, the primary structure being constructed of aluminum alloy. Some non-structural components such as the wing tips and wing strut fairings are made from fiberglass.

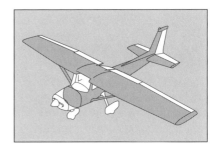

The fuselage has a semi-monocoque structure; that is the vertical bulkheads and frames are joined by horizontal longerons and stringers which run the length of the fuselage. The metal skin is riveted to this structure: this arrangement is conventional for modern light aircraft and allows loads to be spread over the whole construction. At the rear of the fuselage the tail unit consists of a swept fin with rudder and conventional horizontal stabilizer with elevators. Underneath the rear fuselage a metal loop tie-down point/tail guard is fitted. This loop is vulnerable to damage in a "tail strike" and it is possible for it to be pushed back into the fairing at the base of the rudder. The tail guard should be carefully checked during the pre-flight inspection. Small drain holes are drilled in the underneath of the fuselage and at the bottom of the rudder. If water has entered the rear fuselage or rudder, the tail can be lowered to allow the water to drain out.

The tie down/tail guard under the rear fuselage.

The wings are of semi-cantilever design (supported by an external strut) and have a 1° dihedral. At the top of each strut a metal ring is installed to be used as a tie-down point.

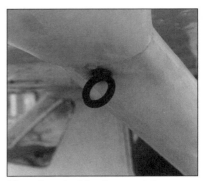

The wing strut tie-down point.

The Flight Controls

Dual flight controls are fitted as standard and link the cockpit controls to the control surface via cable linkages.

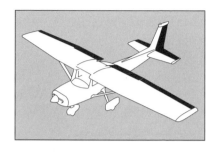

The AILERONS are of the differential type, moving upward through 20° and downward through 15°. Balance weights are incorporated at the lower inner edge of the ailerons, which are of a "frise" design which minimizes adverse yaw.

The FLAPS are slotted, and incorporate Fowler action over the first 10°. They are electrically operated, and can be set between 0° and 30°, compared to the C-150's 40° of flaps. The flaps are controlled by a pre-selectable switch to the right of the mixture control. To select a flap setting the lever is moved to the desired setting—the control is gated in 10° stages—and a small indicator next to the lever shows the actual flap movement.

The gated, pre-selectable flap lever and flap position indicator.

The RUDDER is operated by the rudder pedals (which are also linked to the steerable nose wheel) and can move through 23° either side of the neutral position. On the trailing edge of the control surface, a ground adjustable trim tab is fitted. A horn balance is incorporated in the upper forward portion of the control surface (ahead of the hinge line).

The ELEVATORS move up through 25° and down through 18°. They incorporate a horn balance at their outer forward edge ahead of the hinge line.

The elevator trim tab on the right side elevator, with actuating rod.

An adjustable TRIM TAB is fitted to the right hand elevator. Operation of the cockpit trim wheel (located below the throttle) moves this control surface independently of the elevator control. The trim tab moves through 10° up and 20° down. An indicator mounted next to the cockpit trim wheel shows the trim position set. The control works in the natural sense, i.e., trimming the wheel forward gives nose down trim and vice versa.

The elevator trim wheel and indicator.

The Landing Gear

The 152 landing gear is fixed and is a tricycle-type. The main gear is a tubular steel landing gear strut, surrounded by a full length fairing and fitted with a step. The main gear attaches to the lower fuse-lage, with a plastic fairing where the strut joins the lower fuselage surface. The main gear has a 7' 7" track—the distance between the two main wheels.

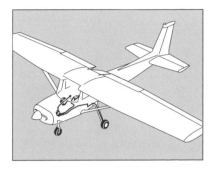

The nose gear attaches to the engine mount and has an air/oil oleo strut to dampen and absorb the normal operating loads. On the rear of the nose strut, a torque link is installed to maintain the correct alignment of the nose wheel; its lower arm is fitted to the nose wheel fork and the upper arm to the oleo cylinder casing. Also fitted to the nose strut is a small cylinder-piston unit, the shimmy damper. This unit reduces nose wheel shimmy (rapid oscillation of the nose wheel, felt as vibration through the rudder pedals) which is most prevalent during takeoff and landing.

The nose gear is steerable through a spring linkage to the rudder pedals. It is steerable through 8° either side of neutral, and can castor under differential braking up to 30°.

The tubular main landing gear leg can absorb heavy loads during taxiing, takeoff and landing.

The braking system consists of single disc brake assemblies fitted to the main landing gear and operated by a hydraulic system. The brakes are operated through the upper portion of each rudder pedal. The pilot's (left hand side) toe brakes have a separate brake cylinder above each pedal; it is possible to operate the brakes differentially—to the left or right wheel. Where co-pilot (right) side pedals are also fitted with toe brakes, they are mechanically linked to the pilot side brake cylinders. The system of toe brakes allows the aircraft to turn in a very tight circle, and it is possible to lock one main wheel with the use of

The nose gear, with the shimmy damper visible.

some toe brake force. Turning around a wheel in this fashion is not recommended as it tends to "scrub" the tire and put excessive pressure on the tire side walls.

A parking brake control is installed on the far left side of the instrument panel. To operate the parking brake the brake pedals are both depressed, and the parking brake knob is pulled out, the pedal pressure is then relaxed and the parking brake control released. The parking brake control is attached to a locking plate which traps pressure in the system while the toe brakes are being activated. The problem is that there may be no apparent visual check to the pilot to show that the brakes are applied. When the aircraft has been parked, it is common practice to try moving the aircraft, to ensure that the parking brake *is* applied. Another problem can arise through the amount of foot force applied by the pilot to operate the brakes, especially when applying the parking brake. If excessive force is used over a period of time, it can lead to fatigue cracks and failures of the rudder bars and seat frames. There are several reported rudder pedal failures on 152s (including at least one during a spinning exercise). The problem of seat failures is covered later in this section.

The main wheels are fitted with 600 X 6 tires as standard, the nose wheel with 500 X 5. The tire grooves should have at least $\frac{1}{16}$" depth over 75% of the tire circumference to be serviceable. Additionally, if the tread across the width of the tire is worn to less than $\frac{1}{16}$" (as might happen if the tire had been "flat spotted" in a skid), in any one place, the tire will need replacing.

The Engine

The 152 is fitted with a Lycoming O-235-L2C engine rated and 110 HP at 2550 RPM up to 1983 models, and an O-235-N2C rated at 108 HP at 2550 RPM from 1983 models on.

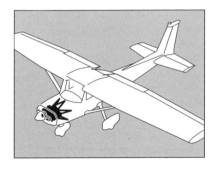

The engine has four cylinders horizontally opposed across the crankshaft. The cylinders are staggered so that each connecting rod has its own crankshaft throw. The cylinder head and crankcase assembly are fashioned from aluminum alloy castings.

The engine is air-cooled. Airflow enters the engine compartment at the front of the cowling, and is directed by baffles to flow over the whole engine. The steel cylinders feature deep fins to aid cooling, the airflow leaves the engine compartment at the lower aft cowling underneath the engine compartment.

The engine is mounted on a steel tubular mounting which attaches to the firewall.

The O-235-N2C engine introduced in 1983 was designed to overcome plug leading problems that affect the L2C version. The N2C features a new combustion chamber with "lead gathering pockets." This appears to work. The lead fouling is reduced on this model and plug life is longer.

The Propeller

The propeller is an all metal, two bladed, fixed pitch design, turned by direct drive from the engine crankshaft. It rotates clockwise as seen from the cockpit and the diameter is 69".

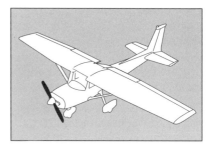

The Cessna 152 propeller.

The Ignition System

The engine features a dual ignition system, fitted with two magnetos. The magnetos are small AC generators which are driven by the crankshaft rotation to provide a very high voltage to a distributor, which directs it via high voltage leads (or high tension leads) to the spark plugs. At the spark plug the current must cross a gap, in doing so a spark is produced which ignites the fuel/air mixture in the cylinder.

The magnetos are fitted at the rear of the engine, one each side of the engine center line (hence, Left and Right magnetos). The usual arrangement is for each magneto to fire one of the two spark plugs in each cylinder, each cylinder has two spark plugs (top and bottom) for safety and efficiency. Apart from 1978 models, both magnetos have impulse couplings, that retard the spark during starting. The leads that run from the magnetos to the spark plugs should be secure and there should be no splits or cracks in the plastic insulation covering the leads.

The ignition system is totally independent of the aircraft electrical system, and once the engine is running it will operate regardless of the battery or alternator.

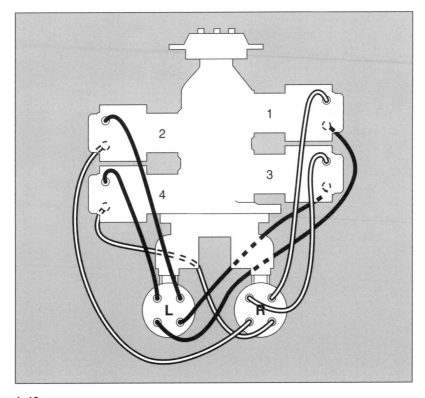

The Oil System

The engine's oil system provides lubrication, cooling, sealing, cleansing and protection against corrosion. The system is a wet-sump, pressure-feed system. The oil sump is located under the engine, and oil is drawn from here through a filter to the engine-driven oil pump. From here a bypass valve sends oil to the oil cooler on the left forward face of the engine, or bypasses it if the oil is cold. The oil then enters the pressure relief valve, and from here goes on to

The oil cooler at the front left side of the engine.

the gallery of the crankcase. If oil pressure is too high, the pressure relief valve routes the excess oil directly back to the sump without passing through the engine. When the oil has flowed around the engine, it drains down to the sump by gravity.

Oil quantity can be checked on a dipstick which is accessible from the upper cowling inspection hatch. The dipstick is graduated in US quarts and measures the quantity of the oil in the sump. When the engine has been running, the oil will take up to 10 minutes to return to the sump, and only then can a true reading be taken. When replacing the dipstick, care should be taken not to over-tighten the cap. To do so may make it exceptionally difficult to reopen and it is possible to strip the thread on the cap or filler tube.

The oil temperature gauge in the cockpit is electrically operated and is linked to a resistance type sender unit in the engine.

The oil pressure gauge reads from a direct pressure oil line to the engine.

The Starter System

The starter motor is housed at the lower front left side of the engine. It incorporates a geared cog that engages with the teeth of the starter ring when the key starter is operated. As the engine is turned an impulse coupling in the left magneto operates, this retards the spark and aids starting; 152 models after 1979 have an impulse coupling on both magnetos. When the engine fires and begins to rotate under its own power, this impulse coupling ceases to operate and normal spark timing is resumed. When the key starter is released, allowing the key to return to the BOTH position, the cog on the starter motor withdraws to be clear of the starter ring.

The Fuel System

The 152 has two aluminum fuel tanks, located one in each wing and joined by a balance pipe. From each tank, a fuel line runs down the inner fuselage to the fuel shut-off valve. From this valve, the fuel line runs to a fuel strainer bowl mounted at the lower firewall and on to the carburetor. A separate line runs from the strainer bowl to the cockpit primer and from there to the cylinder intake ports.

It is essential to visually check the fuel quantity during the pre-flight inspection.

When checking the fuel quantity before flight, it is *vital* to check fuel quantity *visually*—the cockpit fuel gauges are not accurate enough to assess true fuel quantity. Once the fuel quantity has been visually checked, care must be taken to replace the fuel caps securely. When re-fueling, it may be necessary to "top-up" each tank after the initial fueling, as fuel can cross from one tank to the other via the balance pipe—especially if the aircraft is parked on a sloping surface. If the caps are loose or cross-threaded, fuel may vent out from the tank during flight.

The high-wing Cessna singles are often involved in accidents caused by fuel exhaustion. Often the fuel tanks were *not* visually checked during the pre-flight checks, and the fuel ran out even though the gauges were indicating that sufficient fuel remained. The 152 is not unique in being involved in fuel exhaustion accidents; however, its high wing design can lead to a reluctance by the pilot to climb up and visually check the quantity.

The fuel tank vent pipe under the left wing, which must be clean and unblocked.

It is for this reason that the aircraft may be fitted with a step on each wing strut and a grab handle on each side of the upper cowling to aid access to the upper wing.

When the fuel tank levels are low, below 1/4 full for example, prolonged sideslip or skidding maneuvers should be avoided as the tank outlet may be uncovered, and the fuel supply interrupted. For the same reason, extreme "running" takeoffs should also be avoided.

In a gravity feed system positive tank venting is of vital importance. The left tank has a TANK VENT, this is a forward facing pipe on the lower inboard surface of the left wing. The pipe is located directly behind the wing strut to protect it from icing, and it ensures that ambient pressure is maintained above the fuel in the fuel tank. The right hand fuel cap is vented, although some aircraft have vented fuel caps for both fuel tanks. Should the vents become blocked, a depression will form in the tank as the fuel level lowers and fuel flow to the engine may be interrupted.

The fuel strainer drain control is located under the upper cowling inspection hatch. Also visible here is the oil filler pipe.

The fuel shut-off valve on the floor ahead of the seats.

There are usually three FUEL STRAINERS, one at the lower rear inboard edge of each tank, accessible from the inboard lower wing surface, and one located at the fuel strainer bowl. The tank fuel strainers can be used with a fuel tester to collect a fuel sample from each tank. The fuel bowl strainer is operated by a control located under the upper cowling inspection flap. When this control is operated (by pulling) fuel will run from a pipe in the region of the nose strut. To collect fuel from this pipe while operating the drainer can be difficult, but fuel should not be allowed to merely run onto the ground, as this will prove nothing and water or contaminated fuel could go undetected. It is imperative to ensure that the fuel strainer is returned to the OFF position after use, or fuel may continue to drain from the pipe out of view of the pilot.

The fuel shut-off valve is located on the cockpit floor between the forward edges of the seats. The lever is normally in the ON position, lying horizontally. The lever may be safety wired in the ON position, although the FAA now discourages this practice. The lever should be periodically exercised (not in flight!) to check it has not seized. In the event of an emergency requiring the fuel to be turned off, the lever is moved to the vertical position, turning the fuel OFF.

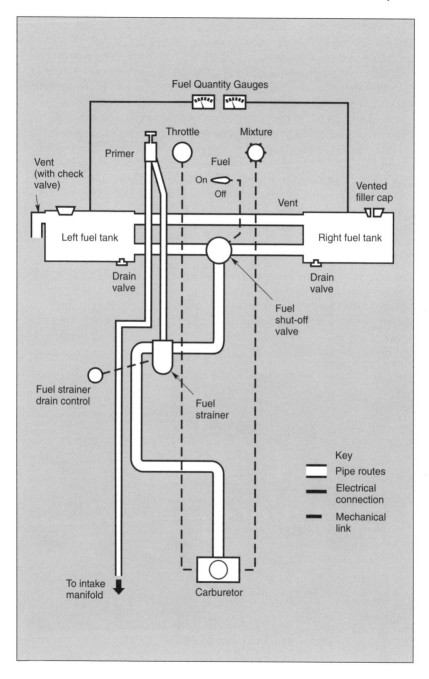

The Carburetor

The CARBURETOR mixes air with the fuel from the fuel system and supplies the fuel/air mix to the cylinders. The up-draft carburetor is located under the engine and takes air from a scoop intake in the lower front cowling. This air is filtered and then fed into the carburetor air box. In this box, a butterfly valve is used to allow either the cold filtered air, or heated air, to be fed to the carburetor. From the carburetor, the induction manifold passes through the oil sump (this is known by Lycoming as the center zone induction manifold). This system allows the fuel/air mix to be warmed by the oil and so ensure uniform vaporization, it also helps to cool the oil. The induction manifold then takes the fuel/air mix to the inlet valve of each cylinder. Heated air comes from an unfiltered inlet at the front cowling which then passes into a shroud around the exhaust which heats it before it reaches the carburetor. Hot or cold air is selected via the carburetor heat control in the cockpit. The use of this control and the subject of carburetor icing is discussed in Section 4.

The 152 models from 1980 on are fitted with an ACCELERATOR PUMP in the carburetor. With a normal carburetor sudden opening of the throttle can cause a momentary lean mixture, causing the engine to hesitate—often at an inopportune moment. The accelerator pump is designed to enrich the mixture momentarily when the throttle is suddenly opened, preventing engine hesitation.

The carburetor heat, throttle and mixture controls.

The PRIMER control situated on the far left of the instrument panel is an aid to starting. The control is unlocked by rotating the control until a pin on the shaft aligns with the cut-out in the collar. The control can then be pulled out, filling the pump with fuel from the fuel strainer. The primer is then pushed in, delivering fuel to the cylinder intake ports. For a cold engine, three cycles on the primer are usually sufficient. When priming is completed the primer should be pushed full in with the pin aligned with the cut-out in the collar, then rotated about half a turn to lock the primer. As a check; attempt to pull the primer out, it should remain locked. It is important that the primer is fully locked, because if it is not, engine rough running may result.

The MIXTURE is controlled from the vernier mixture control located on the lower instrument panel, which adjusts the fuel/air ratio in the carburetor. The mixture control is moved by depressing a button in the center of the control and moving the control IN or OUT. For fine adjustment, the control can be rotated clockwise to enrich the mixture, and counterclockwise to lean the mixture. In the full forward position it gives a RICH mixture, and if moved to the rearward, Idle Cut-Off (ICO) position the fuel supply is cut off and the engine stops.

The THROTTLE is located to the left of the mixture control, it is also of a push/pull type, but does not have the vernier fine adjustment feature of the mixture control. The throttle does have a friction nut at the point where it joins the instrument panel. When this nut is rotated clockwise the throttle movement becomes more difficult, when rotated counterclockwise the throttle movement becomes loose.

The Electrical System

The C152 has a 28 volt, direct current electrical system. The alternator is mounted to the front lower right of the engine and is engine-driven from a belt drive to a ring directly behind the starter ring; the alternator is rated at 60 amps. A 24 volt battery is located inside a vented box on the upper forward right side of the firewall. Depending on the model year and customer option, the battery will be rated between 12.75 ampere-hours and 17 ampere-hours.

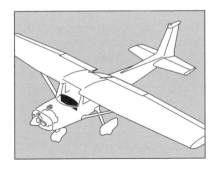

The ALTERNATOR is the primary source of power to the electrical system in normal operations with the engine running. The alternator produces alternating current (AC) which is converted into direct current (DC) by diodes incorporated in the alternator housing which act as rectifiers. By their design, alternators require a small voltage (about 3 volts) to produce the electromagnetic field required inside the alternator. The significance of this is that if the battery is completely discharged (flat), the alternator will not be able to supply any power to the electrical system, even after the engine has been started by some other means (i.e., external power or hand propping). Output from the alternator is controlled by a VOLTAGE REGULATOR mounted on the left side of the firewall. An OVERVOLTAGE SENSOR protects the system from possible damage due to an overvoltage condition. In the event of a high voltage, a relay opens disconnecting the alternator from the electrical system.

The primary purposes of the BATTERY are to provide power for engine starting, the initial excitation of the alternator, and as a backup in the event of alternator failure. In normal operations with the engine running, the alternator provides the power to the electrical system and charges the battery. A fully charged battery has a charging current of about 2 amperes, in a partially discharged condition (i.e., just after engine start) the charging rate can be much higher. In the event of an alternator failure the battery is providing *all* power to the electrical system. In theory, a fully charged 15 ampere hour battery is capable of providing 15 amps for 1 hour, 1 amp for 15 hours, or 7.5 amps for 2 hours, etc. In practice, the power available is governed by factors such as battery age and condition, load placed on it, etc. The best advice is to reduce electrical load to the minimum consistent with safety and plan to make a landing at the earliest opportunity, should an electrical failure occur. Generally the battery can be assumed to have about 30 minutes life in daytime flying.

The AMMETER, located at the far right of the instrument panel, indicates in amperes the electrical current flowing to or from the battery. Should the alternator fail or be shut down, the ammeter will show a discharge, the amount of current flowing from the battery to the electrical system.

With the alternator "off-line," the battery is supplying all power to the electrical system. The high voltage warning light has illuminated and the ammeter is showing a discharge.

The early 152s are fitted with a red HIGH VOLTAGE warning light. Should an over-voltage condition lead to the alternator being shut down, the high voltage light will illuminate to indicate that the battery is supplying all electrical power. In addition, the ammeter will show a discharge. From 1979 models on a red LOW VOLTAGE warning light is installed. Should the voltage fall below approximately 24 volts, the low voltage light will illuminate to indicate a drain on the battery, and the ammeter will show a discharge. It is not unusual for the low voltage light to flicker at low RPMs, especially during taxiing. When a higher RPM is set, the light should go out again.

A low voltage warning light, with "Press to test" facility.

The pilot controls the electrical system via the MASTER SWITCH located on the left side of the instrument panel. This switch is a split rocker switch with two halves, labeled BAT and ALT. Normally the switch is operated as one, both halves being used together. The BAT half of the switch can be operated independently, so that all electrical power is being drawn from the battery only. However, the ALT side can only be turned on in conjunction with the BAT half, for the reasons covered previously. Should an electrical problem occur, the master switch can be used to reset the electrical system by turning it OFF for 2 seconds, and then turning it ON again.

As an option the aircraft may be fitted with an EXTERNAL POWER RECEPTACLE. On the 152, this receptacle is located on the left face of the firewall behind an access door in the side of the cowling. It can be

Here the split master switch has been operated, so that the battery alone is providing power to the electrical system, and the alternator is isolated.

An external power receptacle may be fitted as an option.

used to connect external power for engine starting or operation of the aircraft electrical system. Before using external power it is imperative to check that the external power unit is of the correct voltage—otherwise, *serious damage could be inflicted on the electrical system*. Additionally it should be remembered that if the battery is totally flat (completely discharged), it will need to be removed and recharged or replaced before flight. Cessna recommends that the master switch be turned ON before connecting the external power source, so that any transient voltage can be absorbed by the battery.

The various electrically operated systems are protected by individual CIRCUIT BREAKERS, which are located in a cluster on the lower right instrument panel. Should a problem occur (i.e., a short circuit) the relevant circuit breaker may "pop," and will be raised in relation to the other circuit breakers (CBs). The correct procedure is to allow the CB to cool for 2 minutes, then reset it and check the result. If the CB pops again it should not be reset. The alternator field circuit has a 5 ampere CB, which automatically resets. All CBs show their rating and the components they protect.

Apart from engine starting and alternator field, the electrical system supplies power to the following:

• All internal and external lights.
• All radios and intercom.
• Wing flaps, Pitot heater.
• Turn coordinator.
• Fuel gauges, Oil temperature gauge.

The Stall Warning System

An intake in the left wing leading edge gives an aural stall warning through a horn above the left fresh air control in the cockpit. When the stalling angle of attack is approached, the airflow over the leading edge causes a suction through the reed producing a loud tone, which becomes increasingly high pitched as the stalling angle of attack is reached. Typically, the stall warning activates 5 to 10 KTS above the stall speed.

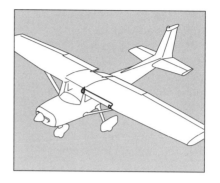

To check the function of the stall warning horn on the ground, the intake should be checked for blockages, and suction can be applied by sucking air through the intake. If this is done it is recommended that a handkerchief or something similar be placed over the intake first to avoid the unpleasant possibility of swallowing any insects stuck in the intake.

The stall warning intake in the left wing leading edge.

The Lighting System

The C152 may be fitted with a variety of optional internal and external lighting. As a general rule, strobes are not used during taxiing as they can dazzle and distract those nearby. They are, however, very effective in the air. If flying in cloud conditions or heavy precipitation, it is recommended that they be turned off as the pilot may become spatially disorientated.

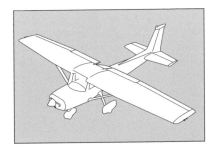

The landing light and taxi lights are fitted in the lower front nose cowling up until 1984 models, after which they are fitted in the left wing leading edge. Again they should be used with some discretion, not least because of the very short life of the light bulbs. There is also an overhead "dome" light located in the cabin ceiling, this light is of a set brightness and has an on/off switch located on its side. The internal lighting will also usually include panel and radio lighting, controlled from a rheostat type control to the left of the rocker switch panel. There may also be a slide switch in the cabin roof console allowing overhead "flood" lighting or door post lighting to be selected. Other options available are a door post map light and a map light on the bottom of the left hand control wheel.

Nose mounted landing light on a pre-1984 152.

The Vacuum System

An engine-driven vacuum pump is mounted to the upper rear face of the engine. This pump is fitted with a plastic shear drive, so that should the pump seize, the drive will shear and the engine will not be damaged. Air enters the vacuum system through a filter, passes through the air-driven gyro instruments (and is measured by the suction gauge), flows through a vacuum regulator and into the vacuum pump, from which it is expelled through a short pipe.

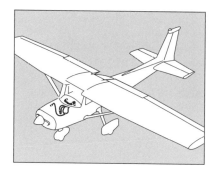

Suction is used to drive the gyros in the attitude indicator (or artificial horizon) and heading indicator (or direction indicator). A gauge mounted on the instrument panel measures suction. For cruising RPMs and altitudes, the reading should be between 4.6 and 5.4 inches of mercury. At higher or lower suction the gyros may become unreliable. A lower suction over an extended period may indicate a faulty vacuum regulator, dirty screens or a system leak. If the vacuum pump fails or a line collapses the suction gauge reading will fall to zero, and the attitude indicator and heading indicator will become unreliable over a period of some minutes as the gyros run down losing RPM. The real danger here is that the effect is gradual and may not be noticed by the pilot for some time. A red LOW VACUUM warning light may be installed on the instrument panel of late model 152s, this light will illuminate if the vacuum drops below 3 inches of mercury.

The Pitot-Static System

The airspeed indicator (ASI), vertical speed indicator (VSI) and altimeter are all connected to the pitot-static system, although the VSI and altimeter use only static pressure and do not have a pitot pressure pick up.

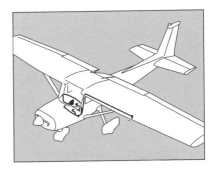

Pitot pressure comes from the PITOT TUBE which is located under the left wing. Static pressure comes from a STATIC VENT located on the forward left fuselage.

No checking facility is incorporated in the system, and instrument indications in the event of a leak or blockage are outside of the scope of this book. As an option, the pitot tube has a heating element which is activated by a switch in the electrical rocker switch group in front of the pilot, labeled PITOT HEAT. Pitot heat can prevent blockage of the pitot tube in heavy rain or icing. This notwithstanding, it must be remembered that *the 152 is not cleared for flight into known icing conditions*.

The pitot tube located under the left wing.

The 152 is not fitted with an alternate static source, so the pressure instruments may become unusable if the normal static vent is blocked. In this instance it is possible to break the face of the VSI, allowing static pressure from the cabin to enter the system. It should be emphasized that this

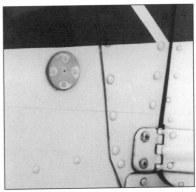

The static vent, on the forward left fuselage.

action is rather drastic (and expensive) and will probably require the use of the blunt end of the fire extinguisher. Action of this type should only be used in a genuine emergency.

The external static vent should be checked before flight to ensure that it is clear and unobstructed. A similar check is carried out on the pitot tube, which may be protected on the ground with a removable pitot cover. It is important not to blow into either pitot tube or static vent, as doing so can result in damage to the pressure instruments.

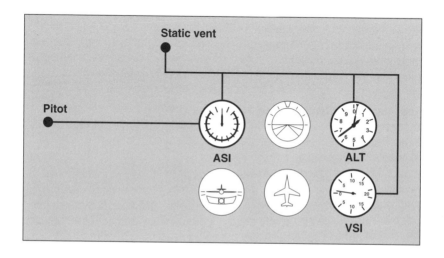

The Heating and Ventilation System

Cabin heating is supplied by a muffler around the engine exhaust system. This allows air, which has entered from an engine baffle inlet, to be warmed by the exhaust pipes. It is then directed to outlets in the footwells and at the lower windscreen. Up to 1980 models a single defrosting outlet is fitted on the left side of the upper glare shield. Post-1980 models have dual (left and right) defrosting outlets fitted as standard. A heating control labeled CABIN HT is mounted next to the flap control. This control is pulled out to select cabin heat and pushed full in to close the shut-off valve at the firewall. A control labeled CABIN AIR directs fresh air through the same outlets as the heated air. Pulling this control out opens a small door in the right forward fuselage. This control can be used individually, or more often to blend with the heated air to provide a comfortable temperature. The heating system is very effective once the engine is warm, although its use is governed by a couple of safety factors.

First, the heating system effectively opens a path through the firewall between the engine compartment and the cockpit. For this reason the cabin heat and defrost are selected OFF before engine start, or if fire is suspected in the engine compartment.

Second, with a system of this type there is always a danger of carbon monoxide (CO) being introduced into the cabin. Carbon monoxide is a gas produced as a by-product of the combustion process. It is colorless, odorless and tasteless, but its effects are potentially fatal and the dangers are widely publicized. A generally accepted practice is to shut off the heating system if engine fumes (which may contain CO) are thought to be entering the cockpit. The danger arises if a crack or split is present in the exhaust system inside the heating shroud, allowing carbon monoxide to enter the heating system.

The ventilation system consists of two cockpit vents, to the extreme right and left of the upper windscreen, which control fresh air from their respective external air intakes located in the inner wing leading edges. The cockpit vents are pulled out to allow fresh air to

An outside air temperature (OAT) gauge is fitted to the right side cockpit air vent.

enter the cockpit, and can be rotated to direct the blast of air they provide. It is generally recommended that the vents be rotated to direct the air onto the inside of the windscreen, rather than directly into the face.

When the heating system is in use it is recommended that the fresh air vents be operated to give a comfortable temperature mix. Doing so will help to combat the possible danger of carbon monoxide poisoning, and will stop the cabin becoming "stuffy" and possibly inducing drowsiness in the pilot.

Seats and Harnesses

The seats may be adjustable 4-way or 6-way. With the standard 4-way seats, fore and aft adjustment is made with a lever located under the front inboard edge of the seat cushion. When this lever is raised the seat can be slid forward or back along the seat tracks until the desired position is reached. The lever should be pushed down and the seat locked in position. The seat back can be adjusted for rake by the use of a knob under the center of the seat. When this control is pulled, the seat back can be adjusted to the desired angle. Both seat backs can be folded forward to aid access to the baggage compartment.

Six-way adjustable seats have a tubular bar under the inboard front seat corner for fore and aft adjustment. A crank at the outboard front corner of each seat can be rotated to adjust seat height, and a lever at the rear inboard corner of each seat is used to adjust the seat back angle.

The seat design of the 152 is subject to criticism in two areas. The first problem arises over the security of the mechanism that locks the seat on the seat rail in the desired fore/aft position. The scenario is that when adjusted the seat fails to lock properly, undetected by the pilot. Then at some stage of flight (often just after takeoff) the seat runs rearward on the rails, taking the occupant with it. The possible consequences—especially if the pilot is flying solo, and if the controls are not released as the seat slides back—can be imagined. Prevention being the best cure, the correct action is to positively ensure that the seat is locked in position, not only after adjustment but also as part of the pre-takeoff checks. The problem is usually well-known to those with some experience on these types, but 30 feet high just after takeoff is not a good place to find out for the first time.

A second problem concerns the seat backs. Fatigue cracking in the seat frames has been the cause of several seat collapses, with the same serious consequences as the seat rail problems. The culprits are usually pilots who apply excessive force on the rudder pedals when using the braking system, especially when applying the parking brake. By pressing hard against the seat back the frame is subject to undue forces. The problem of failing rudder pedals, caused in the same way, was covered on page 1-9.

Harness design may vary between different aircraft. As standard a lap strap will be fitted, with anchor points on the floor, together with a shoulder strap which stows in a plastic channel over the door and anchors to the upper door post. The shoulder strap attaches to the lap strap via a connecting link which clicks onto a stud on the lap strap buckle. As an option, inertia reel harnesses may be fitted, which integrate the lap and shoulder strap. The use of the shoulder straps should be considered mandatory, as upper torso restraint has been shown to be a major factor in accident survivability. Final adjustment of the harness should be done when the seat is in the desired location.

The baggage area behind the seats is sub divided into two sections. Maximum baggage to be carried in this area is 120 lbs, with a maximum of 40 lbs on the rear, sloping section of the compartment. Attention should be drawn to the weight and balance implications of weight in this area. It also must be remembered that for some maneuvers, carrying baggage is prohibited.

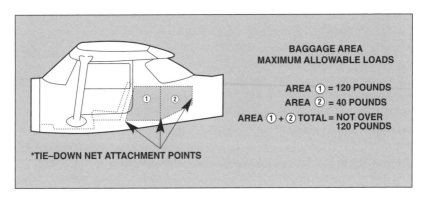

BAGGAGE AREA
MAXIMUM ALLOWABLE LOADS

AREA ① = 120 POUNDS
AREA ② = 40 POUNDS
AREA ① + ② TOTAL = NOT OVER 120 POUNDS

*TIE–DOWN NET ATTACHMENT POINTS

Doors and Windows

The C152 has a door each side of the cabin to allow for easy access. To close the door it is simply pulled shut using the door pull; to check the door is closed properly, pressure should be applied with the hand or elbow. To open the door the recessed door handle is pulled out at its forward edge, the door should open without any extra force being necessary. A door stop is fitted under each wing to prevent overstressing of the door hinges. Aerobats are fitted with jettisonable doors. The door hinge pins are attached to an emergency door release handle mounted on the cabin wall ahead of each door.

The simple "pull to open" door handle of the 152.

The door hinge design of the C152 is apparently prone to cracking, and should be carefully checked during the pre-flight inspection.

Although it is important for the doors to be properly latched for flight, the consequences of partial door opening in flight are usually not serious. If the aircraft is trimmed to approximately 65 knots it should be possible to slam the door shut. Where accidents do occur after a door opens in-flight, they are often caused by pilot distraction rather than as a direct result of the open door.

The window of either door can be opened in flight at any speed up to V_{NE}. The small lever at the center base of the window is moved clockwise a quarter turn to the vertical, and the window opens outward. Each window has a spring-loaded retaining arm that helps to open the window and keep it in the open position. There will be some temporary fluctuations in the readings of the pressure instruments as the window is opened.

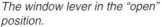

The window lever in the "open" position.

The window lever locking the window closed.

Visibility through the windows can be degraded by oil smears, bugs and other matter accumulating on the windows. For window cleaning a soft cloth and warm, soapy water is recommended. The use of gasoline, alcohol, thinners and window cleaner sprays is not recommended. On the subject of visibility, it is common practice on the 152, as with other high wing aircraft, to lift a wing slightly before a turn in that direction—i.e., lift the left wing a couple of degrees to check for traffic before turning to the left.

Section 2
Limitations

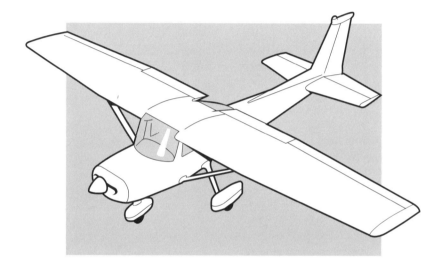

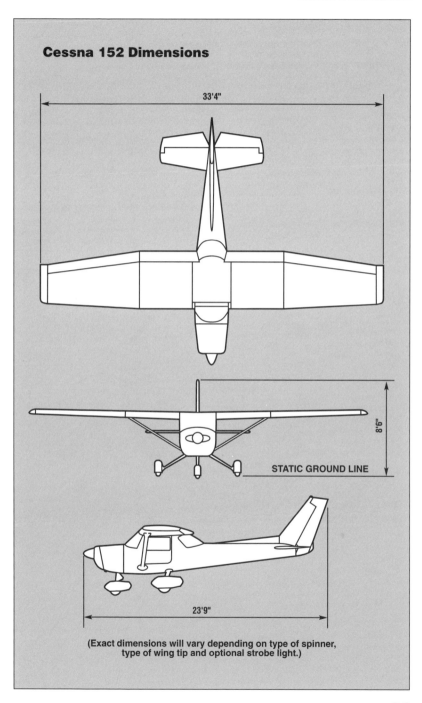

Cessna 152 Dimensions

33'4"

8'6"

STATIC GROUND LINE

23'9"

(Exact dimensions will vary depending on type of spinner,
type of wing tip and optional strobe light.)

The "V" Airspeed Code

V_{S0} – (Low end of white arc) Stalling speed with full flaps.

V_{S1} – (Low end of green arc) Stalling speed without flaps.

V_{FE} – Maximum airspeed with flaps extended. Do not extend flaps above this speed, or fly faster than this speed with any flaps extended.

V_A – Design maneuvering speed. Do not make full or abrupt control movements when flying faster than this speed. Design maneuvering speed should not be exceeded when flying in turbulent conditions.

V_{NO} – Maximum structural cruising speed. Do not exceed this speed except in smooth air conditions.

V_{NE} – Never exceed speed. Do not exceed this airspeed under any circumstances.

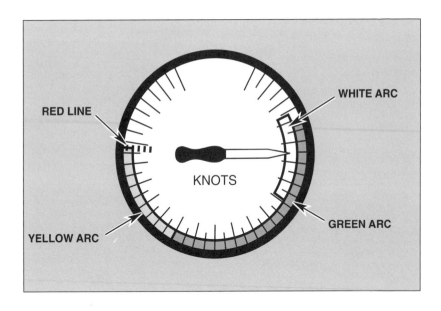

Cessna 152 Limitations

Airspeed Limitations – Cessna 152
(all quoted speeds are INDICATED airspeed-IAS)

	Knots	**MPH**
V_{NE}	149	171
V_{NO}	111	128
V_A (at 1670 lbs)	104	120
V_A (at 1500 lbs)	98	113
V_A (at 1350 lbs)	93	107
V_{FE}	85	98
Stalling Speed clean	40	46
Stalling Speed Full Flaps	35	40

Airspeed Indicator Markings – Cessna 152

	Knots	**MPH**
RED LINE (Never Exceed)	149	171
YELLOW ARC (Caution range)	111 – 149	128 – 171
GREEN ARC (Normal operating range)	40 – 111	46 – 128
WHITE ARC (Flap extended range)	35 – 85	40 – 98

Airframe Limitations – Cessna 152

Weights	**Lbs**
Maximum Ramp Weight	1675
Maximum Takeoff Weight	1670
Maximum Landing Weight	1670
Maximum Baggage Weight	120

Note: the baggage compartment must be empty for aerobatic maneuvers.

Flight Load Factors – Cessna 152
Maximum Positive load factor:

FLAPS UP	4.4G
FLAPS DOWN	3.5G

Maximum Negative load factor:

FLAPS UP	-1.76
FLAPS DOWN	0

Airspeed Limitations – Cessna 152 Aerobat
(quoted speeds are INDICATED airspeed—IAS)

	Knots	MPH
V_{NE}	172	198
V_{NO}	125	144
V_A	108	124
V_{FE}	85	98
Stalling Speed clean	40	46
Stalling Speed Full Flaps	35	40

Airspeed Indicator Markings – Cessna 152 Aerobat

	Knots	MPH
RED LINE (Never Exceed)	172	198
YELLOW ARC (Caution range)	125 – 172	144 – 198
GREEN ARC (Normal operating range)	40 – 125	46 – 144
WHITE ARC (Flap extended range)	35 – 85	40 – 98

Flight Load Factors – Cessna 152 Aerobat
Maximum Positive load factor:

FLAPS UP	+6.0G
FLAPS DOWN	+3.5G

Maximum Negative load factor:

FLAPS UP	-3.0G
FLAPS DOWN	0

Maximum Demonstrated
Crosswind Component   12 Knots

Performance Limitations
    Service Ceiling – 14,700 ft

Engine Limitations

	Tachometer	Instrument Marking
Maximum RPM	2550	Red Line
Normal Operating Range	1900 – 2550	Green Arc

	Oil Temperature	Instrument Marking
Normal operating range	100° – 245°F	Green Arc
Maximum	245°F / 118°C	Red Line

	Oil Pressure	Instrument Marking
Normal operating range	60 – 90 psi	Green Arc
Minimum	25 psi	Red Line
Maximum	100* psi	Red Line

(*115 psi on some aircraft – check flight manual)

Oil Quantity

	US quart
Sump Capacity	6
Minimum safe quantity	4

Fuel System

Fuel Quantity—Standard Tanks	US Gal
Total Capacity	26
Unusable Fuel	1.5
Usable Fuel (all flight conditions)	24.5

Cessna 152 A Pilot's Guide

Miscellaneous Limitations

		Tire
Nose Wheel Tire Pressure	30 psi	5.00 X 5
Main Wheel Tire Pressure	21 psi	6.00 X 6

Oil Grades

Lycoming approves lubricating oil for the engine that conforms to specification MIL-L-6082 (straight mineral type) and specification MIL-L-22851 (ashless dispersant type).

Straight mineral oil is usually only used when the engine is new, or after maintenance work on the engine. Straight oil grades are known by their weight.

Ashless dispersant oils are more commonly used in service. Ashless dispersant type oil must not be used when the engine is operating on straight mineral oil. It is therefore very important to check which type of oil is currently being used in the engine and be sure to only add the same type.

Both types of oil are available in different grades, used according to the average surface air temperature. The recommended grades are set out as SAE numbers. The tables below show the recommended grades for various surface temperature bands.

O-235-N2C ENGINE

AVERAGE SURFACE AIR TEMPERATURE	MIL-L-6082 Straight mineral
Above 60°F / 16°C	SAE 50
30°F / -1°C – 90°F / 32°C	SAE 40
0°F / -18°C – 70°F / 21°C	SAE 30
AVERAGE SURFACE AIR TEMPERATURE	**MIL-L-22851 Ashless Dispersant**
Above 60°F / 16°C	SAE 50
30°F / -1°C – 90°F / 32°C	SAE 40
0°F / -18°C – 70°F / 21°C	SAE 30

O-235-L2C ENGINE

AVERAGE SURFACE AIR TEMPERATURE	MIL-L-6082 Straight mineral
Above 60°F / 16°C	SAE 50
30°F / -1°C – 90°F / 32°C	SAE 40
0°F / -18°C – 70°F / 21°C	SAE 30
Below 10°F / -12°C	SAE 20
AVERAGE SURFACE AIR TEMPERATURE	**MIL-L-22851 Ashless Dispersant**
Above 60°F / 16°C	SAE 50 or SAE 40
30°F / -1°C – 90°F / 32°C	SAE 40
0°F / -18°C – 70°F / 21°C	SAE 30 or SAE 40
Below 10°F / -12°C	SAE 30

Fuel Grades

The Cessna 152 is certified for use with 100LL fuels. In fact, one of the major reasons for the introduction of the 152 with its Lycoming engine was the gradual introduction of 100LL fuels.

The table below shows the recommended fuel grades. It is wise to pay attention when your aircraft is being refueled, especially if away from your usual airfield. More than one pilot has found out to their cost that piston engines designed for AVGAS do not run very well on turbine fuel (Jet A-1). To help guard against this eventuality AVGAS fueling points carry a RED sticker and turbine fuel fueling points a BLACK sticker. The C152 with the L2C engine may use automobile gasoline in accordance with detailed procedure restrictions and limitations set out by the STC requirement.

APPROVED FUEL GRADES
100LL 100L 100 (formerly 100/130)

Section 3
Handling the Cessna 152

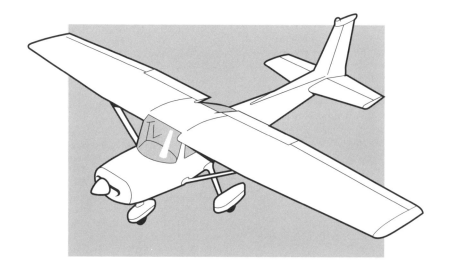

Note: The information in this section is no substitute for flight instruction under the guidance of a flight instructor familiar with the aircraft and its characteristics.

Ground Handling

Whenever possible, a towbar should be used for manually maneuvering the aircraft. The towbar attaches to the nose wheel assembly and provides a point to push or pull as well as allowing accurate steering. When using a towbar, take care not to exceed the nose wheel turning angle limit of 30°.

Unfortunately, a towbar is not always available when you need it. In this case, the push/pulling points are the wing strut ends and landing gear struts. Using the propeller to pull or push is not recommended— bearing in mind that it is virtually impossible to be sure that the propeller is not "live"—even if the key is out of the magneto switch. The leading edge of the horizontal stabilizer *must not* be used as a pushing point—there are recorded cases of structural damage to the horizontal stabilizer caused by incorrect ground handling. To steer the aircraft without a towbar, the tail must be lowered to raise the nose wheel clear of the ground, the aircraft can then be pivoted about the main wheels. The tail can be lowered by pushing down over the horizontal stabilizer front spar adjacent to the fuselage, or over a rear fuselage bulkhead. *Do not* push down on the outer horizontal stabilizer or on the control surfaces. The aircraft flight instructor or operator should be able to point out the correct push down points.

Engine Starting

Starting the C152 is uncomplicated, the ambient conditions and engine temperature being the principle factors to be considered. Somewhere between 1 and 3 primes are required for starting; generally the colder the ambient temperature and engine temperature, the more priming will be required. The throttle is set to one-quarter open (that is, 1/4-inch in). "Pumping" of the throttle, especially during starting, should be avoided as the accelerator pump in the carburetor (1980 models and later) can cause fuel to pool in the intake, leading to a fire risk. On the earlier models without an accelerator pump, "pumping" of the throttle is useless as it will only cause an excessively lean mixture.

Early model O-235-L2C engines can sometimes prove difficult to start. Lycoming has issued a service instruction with a recommended starting procedure if experiencing starting problems: after normal priming, the primer is left OUT after the last primer stroke. The throttle is set 1/2" open. As the engine starts the primer is pushed in, the throttle is advanced to keep the engine running, and then the primer is locked closed.

Later model L2C engines, and N2C model engines, have a slower turning engine starter, which makes engine starting easier. Cranking of the starter should be limited to 30 seconds at a time due to the danger of the starter motor overheating. That said, 30 seconds is a bit extreme, and if the engine does not fire within 10-15 seconds you can reasonably suppose that something is amiss (usually the engine is over or under-primed). After a prolonged period of engine cranking without a successful start, the starter should be allowed a few minutes to cool before a further attempt is made. The starter should not be operated after engine start, as damage to the starter may result.

After start, the oil pressure should register within 30 seconds (or slightly longer in very cold conditions); should the oil pressure not register the engine should be shut down without delay. Readings on the suction gauge and ammeter are also usually checked after engine start.

Starting With a Suspected Flooded Engine

An over-primed (flooded) engine will be indicated by weak intermittent firing, and puffs of black smoke from the exhaust during the attempted start. If it is suspected that the engine is flooded (over-primed) the throttle should be opened fully and the mixture moved to idle cut off. If the engine starts, the throttle should be retarded to the normal position and the mixture moved to full rich.

Starting In Cold Ambient Conditions (below 0°C)

Failure to start due to an under-primed engine is more likely to occur in cold conditions with a cold engine. An under-primed engine will not fire at all, and additional priming will be necessary. Starting in cold temperatures will be more difficult due to several factors: the oil will be more viscous, the battery may lose up to half of its capacity and the fuel will not vaporize readily. A greater number of primes will be required, and external power may be needed to supplement the aircraft battery. Pre-heat may be necessary in very low temperatures.

Starting In Hot Ambient Conditions

There are few problems associated with engine starting in high temperatures. The main problem concerns fuel vaporization after the engine has been running. After the engine is shut down the temperature of the various engine components will stabilize, some cooling some heating. The fuel system tends to heat up, and fuel in the lines may "boil" or vaporize. This vapor will inhibit starting until the entire fuel system is filled with liquid fuel. This problem is generally worse between 30 and 60 minutes after engine shut down. The only real solution is to allow time for the fuel system to cool, and to open the throttle slightly more than usual when starting.

Taxiing

In the first few feet of taxiing, a brake check is normally carried out, followed by steering and differential brake checks in due course. To anyone used to aircraft with "direct" steering rods from the rudder pedals to the nose wheel, the spring link system of the 152 may at first seem very "loose" and inexact.

It should be remembered that the rudder pedals only steer the nose wheel through 10° either side of neutral, and differential braking is required to castor the nose wheel up to its limit of 30°. The 152 is easy to taxi, although practice may be needed in the increased use of the rudder pedals and differential braking when taxiing in crosswind conditions.

Cessna 152 A Pilot's Guide

When taxiing with a crosswind, "opposite rudder" will be required, up to full deflection (i.e. with a crosswind from the left, up to full right rudder) may be required as the aircraft tries to "weathervane" into the wind.

The figure below shows recommended control column positions when taxiing with the prevailing wind from the directions shown.

Speed control is important, especially when taxiing over rough surfaces or in strong wind conditions. When slowing the aircraft, the throttle should always be closed first, then the brakes evenly applied. If taxiing over loose stones or gravel the RPM should be kept to a minimum to avoid damage to the propeller.

Prolonged idling (below about 800 RPM) should be avoided during ground operations as it can lead to plug fouling.

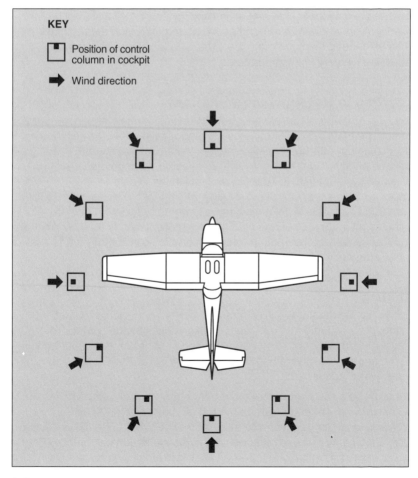

Power and Pre-Takeoff Checks

The aircraft is usually positioned into the wind to aid engine cooling. Before starting the power check, the oil temperature should be in the green arc.

The engine is generally run up to 1,700 RPM when the carburetor heat is checked, a small drop in RPM should result. The subject of carburetor icing is covered more fully in Section 4, however an important point to note is that the inlet for the "hot" air is unfiltered. Therefore, dust, grass, etc. may well enter the engine when "hot" air is selected, leading to increased engine wear. For this reason the use of carburetor heat should be kept to the minimum necessary while on the ground.

The magnetos are checked individually. A small drop in RPM (not more than 125 RPM) is the norm and shows that the ignition system is functioning properly. No drop at all in RPM, when operating on one magneto, may well indicate a malfunction in the ignition system, and the possibility of one or both magnetos staying "live." The difference in RPM between each magneto operating singly should not be more than 50 RPM. An excessive drop in RPM when operating on one magneto, especially when accompanied by rough running, may indicate fouled spark plugs or a faulty magneto. If fouled plugs are suspected it may be possible to clear the problem. The engine should be advanced to about 2,000 RPM with magnetos on BOTH and the mixture leaned to give the "peak" RPM. This should be held for about 10 seconds, then the mixture returned to full rich, power brought back to 1,700 RPM and the magnetos can be rechecked.

> **WARNING:** Excessive power setting and over-lean mixture settings should be avoided during this procedure. If the problem does not clear, the aircraft should be considered unserviceable.

The engine gauges, together with the suction gauge and ammeter, are checked at 1,700 RPM for normal indications.

Engine idling is also checked; with the throttle closed the engine should run smoothly at about 500 to 750 RPM.

During the pre-takeoff checks two items are of particular importance to the 152. First, the flap settings should always be visually checked. Problems with the flap operating system have led to instances of 152s attempting takeoff with full flaps, even though only 10° of flaps was set. Second, the seat locking must be carefully checked, due to the seat security problems already mentioned in Section 1.

Takeoff

Normally, takeoff is made with the mixture in the full RICH position. At high elevation airfields (above 3,000 feet MSL) it may be necessary to lean the mixture before beginning the takeoff to obtain full power.

For all takeoffs, care must be taken to ensure that the feet remain clear of the toe brakes. This is best done by keeping the heels on the floor. Inadvertent pressure on the toe brakes can significantly slow the aircraft during the takeoff run and lead to directional control difficulties.

At the start of the takeoff run (as at all other times), the throttle should be opened smoothly and progressively. Rapid opening of the throttle should be specifically avoided. The normal rotation speed is around 50 knots, with a climb speed of 65 knots dependent on conditions and operator procedures. The best rate-of-climb airspeed is 67 knots IAS. For "short field" takeoffs the use of 10° of flaps is recommended. Flap settings beyond 10° must not be used for takeoff as the increased lift is matched by a larger increase in drag and is therefore counterproductive. After takeoff, an airspeed of 54 knots gives the best angle-of-climb airspeed with 10° flaps. Flaps should not be retracted until the airspeed has reached 60 knots.

Particularly on rough surfaces, it is important to protect the nose wheel through use of the elevator by keeping weight off it during the takeoff run. Care should be taken to avoid "over-rotating" during the takeoff run as this will lengthen the takeoff run, and ruin the view ahead!

Climbing

While climbing it is important to monitor the engine gauges, as the engine is operating at a high power setting but with reduced cooling airflow compared to cruising flight. Lookout ahead is impaired by the high nose attitude and it is common practice to "weave" the nose periodically during the climb to visually check the area ahead.

The recommended best rate-of-climb airspeed reduces as altitude increases. By 10,000 feet it has become 61 knots IAS.

Cruising Flight

Cruising is normally done with a power setting of 55 – 75%. Typically a setting of 2,150 RPM will give an indicated airspeed of around 95 knots.

If turbulent conditions are encountered in flight, particular care must be taken not to exceed V_A (Design Maneuvering Airspeed). V_A for a C152 at maximum-gross weight is 104 knots, reducing as weight is reduced:

1670 lbs – 104 knots

1500 lbs – 98 knots

1350 lbs – 93 knots

152 Aerobats have a V_A of 108 knots—check the airplane flight manual.

Engine Handling

Engine rough-running and engine failure can be caused by a number of factors. Sadly, the majority of engine failures in light aircraft are due to pilot error. After carburetor icing, fuel exhaustion (running out of fuel) is the most common cause of engine failures on 152s. Having sufficient fuel on board to complete the flight is a point of basic airmanship. Avoid running out of fuel by proper flight planning and thorough pre-flight checks—especially a VISUAL fuel quantity check.

Regular monitoring of the engine instruments may forewarn of an impending problem. HIGH OIL TEMPERATURE, if not accompanied by a corresponding drop in oil pressure, may indicate a faulty gauge. As with most instances the action to be taken will depend on the pilots judgment of the situation at the time. A reasonable course of action would be a diversion to a suitable airfield, while remaining alert to the possibility of a sudden engine failure. *Where high oil temperature is accompanied by low oil pressure, engine failure may very well be imminent and the pilot should act accordingly.* Such a situation might occur during a prolonged slow climb in hot conditions; in this instance increasing the airspeed to provide more cooling and reducing power if possible may restore oil temperature to normal. In the event of a LOW OIL PRESSURE reading, accompanied by a normal oil temperature reading, again gauge failure may be the culprit, and the pilot can consider actions similar to those for an oil temperature gauge failure. Where the low oil pressure is accompanied by a high oil temperature, engine failure could well be imminent and the pilot will want to act accordingly.

Stalling

Note: *The information in this section is no substitute for flight instruction under the guidance of a flight instructor familiar with the aircraft and its characteristics.*

The 152 is conventional in its stalling behavior. The stall warning horn activates 5 to 10 knots above the stall airspeed. The airspeed indicator is unreliable at very slow airspeeds and tends to under-read considerably. The airspeed indicator (ASI) is marked in indicated airspeed (IAS); close to the stall airspeed IAS varies considerably from Calibrated or Rectified Airspeed (CAS/RAS)—which is IAS corrected for position error. At an INDICATED stalling speed of 40 knots the CAS/RAS is nearer 48 knots. Flight manuals for later model 152s have tables giving stall speeds at forward and rearward Center of Gravity positions. The use of power will lower the stalling speed, while turning flight raises the stalling speed. With the flaps down some elevator buffeting occurs prior to the stall. The use of flaps, power, or turning flight considerably increases the chances of a wing drop at the stall. When practicing stalls, the possibility of a wing drop can be reduced by keeping the aircraft in balance during the approach to the stall. Typical height loss for a full stall with a conventional recovery (using power) is about 150 feet.

Spins

Note: *The information in this section is no substitute for flight instruction under the guidance of a flight instructor familiar with the aircraft and its characteristics.*

Cessna has produced a detailed supplement covering spin characteristics and recovery procedures for Cessna single-engined aircraft; this is recommended reading.

The Cessna 152 is approved for intentional spinning, however:

INTENTIONAL SPINS WITH FLAPS EXTENDED ARE PROHIBITED.

In addition, no baggage is to be carried.

As with stalling, several factors can affect the behavior of the aircraft in the spin. It is quite possible to devote a whole book just to this subject, and it is not the intention here to write a textbook on spinning. However, some points are worthy of mention. The weight of the aircraft (and particularly the CG position) has a noticeable effect on the spin; a forward CG position makes a pure spin more difficult to obtain, a spiral with increasing airspeed and "g" loads is more likely. With aft CG positions the spin is easier to achieve, and recoveries may take longer. High weights tend to extend the spin recovery due to the increase in inertia. The use of power in the spin tends to lead to a "flatter" spin attitude, and recoveries may be lengthened. Finally, the position of the ailerons is important in spinning. The ailerons should be held NEUTRAL throughout the spin and recovery.

Cessna recommends that spin entry is best accomplished by leading with full rudder in the desired spin direction just prior to the application of full up elevator. During the spin entry, the aircraft may well pitch through the vertical attitude in the first turn. The rate of rotation then increases with the nose attitude becoming $65° - 75°$ after two turns. If the spin is continued beyond two turns the load factor tends to increase, and with forward CG positions spiral tendencies may become evident with the airspeed rising and increased "g" loading. It must be emphasized that this very general description is dependent on many factors as already discussed. Recovery from the spin can be summarized as follows:

• Check ailerons neutral and throttle idle.

• Apply and maintain full opposite rudder (opposite to the direction of spin).

• Just after the rudder reaches the stop move the control wheel forward and hold this position until the stall is broken and the spin stops.

• When rotation stops, neutralize the rudder and recover from the ensuing dive.

In the early stages of the spin (first two turns approximately) recovery can be almost instantaneous, especially at forward CG positions. Once in the steady spin, recovery is more likely to take up to 1 turn. In all spinning it is important to ensure that the proper recovery actions are taken and that the recovery control positions are held until recovery occurs.

Descent

The descent may be powered or glide. For the glide, a speed of 60 knots is recommended. Where flaps are used, the rate of descent increases markedly. The initial lowering of flaps leads to a distinct nose up pitching and reduced airspeed. Especially at airspeeds close to V_{FE} the trim change can be quite marked and the aircraft may "balloon" while the attitude is changed and the aircraft re-trimmed.

The low power settings usually used during the descent and a possible prolonged descent into warmer air, provide ideal conditions for carburetor icing. Full carburetor heat should be used where necessary. In a glide descent, power should be added for short periods throughout the descent to help prevent spark plug fouling, rapid cylinder cooling, and of course, carburetor icing.

Landing

The Cessna 152 is almost universally described as being an easy aircraft
to land. This does not prevent the Cessna 152 (as with many other light
aircraft) from appearing year after year in landing accident reports.
Whether this is due to the aircraft design itself, or due to the very high
numbers of these trainers in service, is open to discussion. It is rare
that anybody is hurt in these accidents, but the reports seem surpris-
ingly similar:

"Cessna F152 ——. Nose gear collapsed and the aircraft was exten-
sively damaged during a series of bounces while landing...."

"Cessna 152 ___. Following a misjudged landing at ————, the aircraft
bounced and the nose gear collapsed."

"Cessna 152 ——. While attempting to land on runway 29 ...... the
aircraft touched down heavily after drifting to the left of the runway and
the nose gear collapsed."

"Cessna A152 —. Nose gear collapsed following several bounces on
landing at ——."

As already mentioned, the nose wheel is nowhere near as strong as the
main landing gear, but there is no need for its strength to be tested if a
proper approach and landing technique is used. Normal approach speed
with flaps is about 65 knots, usually a little higher for a flapless approach,
dependent on conditions and operator procedures. For a short field
approach, full flaps and an approach speed of 54 knots is recommended.

Incorrect approach speed is a primary cause of "ballooning," which often
leads to bouncing. Bouncing also occurs where the aircraft is allowed to
touch down at too high a speed, usually in a level attitude rather than a
nose up attitude. The correct action in either a "balloon" or a bounce is to
GO AROUND without delay. The correct landing technique is to approach
at the proper speed, "flare" or "hold off," close the throttle, and gradually
raise the nose to ensure a low touch down speed on the MAINWHEELS
FIRST, with the nose wheel still off the ground. As the aircraft slows down,
correct use of the elevators means the nose wheel is allowed to gently
contact the surface some time after the initial mainwheel contact. Again,
there is no substitute for flight instruction in the proper technique with a
flight instructor.

The correct landing attitude may be more difficult to achieve when full flaps are extended; the aircraft will tend to land "flat." In a glide approach with full flaps the high rate of descent and large change in attitude required to flare takes some getting used to.

One of the significant airframe modifications between the 150 and 152 was the reduction in maximum flap setting from 40° to 30°. This was not universally welcomed, as in the right hands 40° of flaps on the 150 could prove very useful at times. However, limiting the flaps to 30° and introducing the "gated" flap lever does simplify the full flap go-around. The go-around with full flaps in the 152 is characterized by a considerable trim change when full power is applied, and some pilots may have difficulty in holding the attitude required until able to use the elevator trim to reduce the control force. One of the immediate actions in the go-around is to raise the flaps to 20° to improve climb performance over the full flaps climb. The "gated" flap lever design of the 152 makes this far easier than in the 150s.

Parking and Tie Down

The aircraft is generally parked into the wind. It is good practice to stop with the nose wheel straight so that the rudder is not deflected. All switches should be off, the doors closed and the control wheel lock fitted. In extremely cold weather it may be advisable *not* to set the parking brake as moisture may freeze the brakes; in addition the parking brake should not be set if there is reason to believe that the brakes are over-heated. If for any reason the parking brake is not set, the wheels should be "chocked."

When strong winds are forecast, all possible precautions should be taken.

When tying down the aircraft, the following technique is recommended:

• Park the aircraft into the wind with the control wheel lock in.

• Ropes, cables or chains are attached to the wing tie-down points and secured to ground anchor points.

• If desired, a rope (not cable or chain) can be secured to the exposed portion of the engine mount and secured to a ground anchor point.

• A rope can be passed through the tail tie-down point and each end secured at a 45° angle to the ground either side of the tail.

• Fitting of external control locks (particularly to the rudder) may be advisable in strong or gusty wind conditions.

It is also prudent to use a pitot cover, particularly if the aircraft will be left unattended for some time.

Section 4
Mixture and Carburetor Icing Supplement

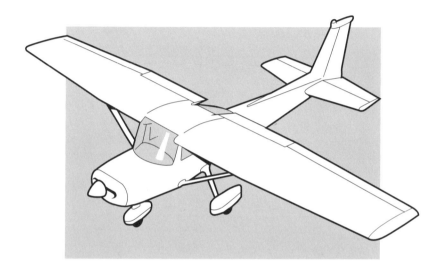

Carburetor Icing

Almost certainly the most common cause of engine rough running, and complete engine failure, is carburetor icing. Despite this, carburetor icing remains a widely misunderstood subject. Many pilots' knowledge of the subject is limited to a feeling that the carburetor heat should be used regularly in flight, without really knowing the symptoms of carburetor icing or the conditions most likely to cause its formation.

How Carburetor Icing Forms

IMPACT ICING occurs when ice forms over the external air inlet (air filter) and inside the induction system leading to the carburetor. This type of icing occurs with the temperature below 0°C while flying in a cloud, or in precipitation (i.e., rain, sleet or snow). These conditions are also conducive to airframe icing, and this aircraft is *not cleared for flight into known icing conditions,* which clearly these are. So, assuming the aircraft is operated legally within its limitations, this form of icing should not occur, and is not considered further.

CARBURETOR ICING is caused by a temperature drop inside the carburetor, which can happen even in conditions where other forms of icing will not occur. The causes of this temperature drop are twofold:

1. Fuel icing—the evaporation of fuel inside the carburetor. Liquid fuel changes to fuel vapor and mixes with the induction air causing a large temperature drop. If the temperature inside the carburetor falls below 0°C, water vapor in the atmosphere condenses into ice, usually on the walls of the carburetor passage adjacent to the fuel jet, and on the throttle valve. Generally, fuel icing is responsible for around 70% of the temperature drop in the carburetor.

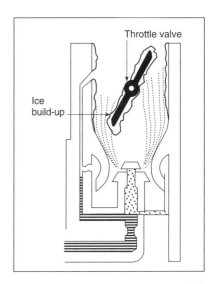

2. Throttle icing—the temperature loss caused by the acceleration of air and consequent pressure drop around the throttle valve. This effect may again take the temperature below 0°C and water vapor in the inlet air will condense into ice on the throttle valve. This practical effect is a demonstration of Bernoulli's Principle.

   As fuel and throttle icing generally occur together, they are known just as carburetor icing.

Carburetor Icing Conditions

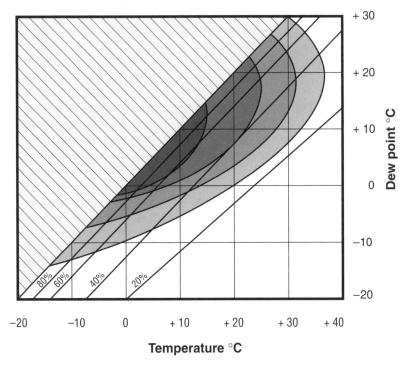

Temperature °C

100% Relative humidity

Serious icing – any power

Moderate icing – cruise power
Serious icing – descent power

Serious icing – descent power

Light icing – cruise or descent power

Conditions Likely to Lead to Carburetor Icing

Two criteria govern the likelihood of carburetor icing conditions: the AIR TEMPERATURE and the RELATIVE HUMIDITY.

The ambient air temperature is important, *but not because the temperature needs to be below 0°C, or even close to freezing.* This temperature drop in the carburetor can be up to 30°C, so carburetor icing can (and does) occur in hot ambient conditions. It is no wonder carburetor icing is sometimes referred to as refrigeration icing. Carburetor icing is considered a possibility within the temperature range of -10°C to +30°C.

The relative humidity (a measure of the water content of the atmosphere) is a major factor. The greater the water content in the atmosphere (the higher the relative humidity), the greater the risk of carburetor icing. That said, the relative humidity (RH) does not have to be 100% (i.e., visible water droplets—clouds, rain) for carburetor icing to occur. Carburetor icing is considered a possibility at relative humidity values as low as 30%. Herein lies the real danger of carburetor icing, that it can occur in such a wide range of conditions. Obviously the pilot must be alert to the possibility of carburetor icing at just about all times. Flight in or near clouds or in other visible moisture (i.e., rain) might be an obvious cause of carburetor icing, but *visible moisture does not need to be present for carburetor icing to occur.*

Symptoms of Carburetor Icing

In this aircraft, fitted with a fixed pitch propeller, the symptoms of carburetor icing are straightforward. A loss of RPM will be the first symptom, although this is often first noticed as a loss of altitude. As the icing becomes more serious, engine rough running may occur.

Carburetor icing is often detected during the use of carburetor heat. Normally when the carburetor heat is used, a small drop in RPM occurs; when the control is returned to cold (off), the RPM restores to the same as before the use of carburetor heat. If the RPM restores to a higher figure than before the carburetor heat was used, it can be assumed that some form of carburetor icing was present.

Use of Carburetor Heat

Apart from the normal check of carburetor heat during power checks, it may be necessary to use the carburetor heat on the ground if carburetor icing is suspected. Safety considerations apart, the use of carburetor heat on the ground should be kept to a minimum, because the hot air inlet is unfiltered, and sand or dust can enter the engine, increasing engine wear.

Carburetor icing is generally considered to be very unlikely with the engine operating at above 75% power, i.e., during the takeoff and climb. Carburetor heat should not be used with the engine operating at above 75% power (i.e., full throttle) as detonation may occur. Detonation is the uncontrolled burning of fuel in the cylinders, literally an explosion, and will cause serious damage to the engine very quickly. Apart from the danger of detonation, the use of carburetor heat reduces the power the engine produces. In any situation where full power is required (i.e., takeoff, climb, go-around) the carburetor heat must be off (cold).

Very few operators recommend the use of anything other than FULL carburetor heat. A normal carburetor icing check will involve leaving the carburetor heat on (hot) for 5 to 10 seconds, although the pilot may wish to vary this, dependent on the conditions. The use of carburetor heat does increase fuel consumption, and this may be a factor to consider if the aircraft is being flown towards the limit of its range/endurance in possible carburetor icing conditions.

With carburetor icing present, the use of carburetor heat may lead to a large drop in RPM, with rough running. The instinctive reaction is to put the carburetor heat back to cold (off), and quickly. This is, however, the wrong action. Chances are this rough running is a good thing, and the carburetor heat should be left on (hot) until the rough running clears and the RPM rises. In this instance, the use of carburetor heat has melted a large amount of accumulated ice and the melted ice is passing through the engine causing temporary rough running.

Care should be taken when flying in very cold ambient conditions (below -10°C). In these conditions the use of carburetor heat may actually raise the temperature in the carburetor to that most conducive to carburetor

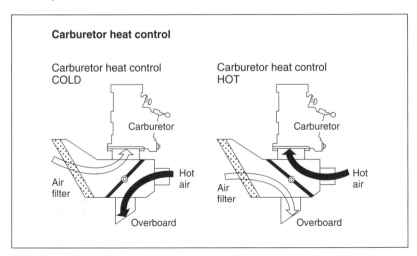

Carburetor heat control

Carburetor heat control
COLD

Carburetor

Air
filter

Hot
air

Overboard

Carburetor heat control
HOT

Carburetor

Air
filter

Hot
air

Overboard

icing. Generally, when the temperature in the carburetor is below -8°C, moisture forms directly into ice crystals which pass through the engine.

The RPM loss normally associated with the use of carburetor heat is caused by the reduced density of the hot air entering the carburetor, leading to an over-rich mixture entering the engine. If the carburetor heat has to be left constantly on (hot)—i.e., flight in heavy rain and clouds—it may be advisable to lean the mixture in order to maintain RPM and smooth engine running.

It is during the descent (and particularly the glide descent) that carburetor icing is most likely to occur. The position of the throttle valve (i.e., almost closed) is a contributory factor, and even though the carburetor heat is normally applied throughout a glide descent, the low engine power will reduce the temperature of the hot air selected with the carburetor heat control. In addition, a loss of power may not be readily noticed. The propeller is likely to windmill even after a complete loss of power, so a full loss of power may only be apparent when the throttle is opened at the bottom of the descent. This is one good reason for opening the throttle to "clear the engine" at intervals during a glide descent.

The Mixture Control

The aircraft is provided with a mixture control so that the pilot can adjust the fuel/air mixture entering the engine. The cockpit mixture control operates a needle valve between the float bowl and the main metering jet. This valve controls the fuel flow to the main metering jet to adjust the mixture. With the mixture control in the idle cut-off position (full lean), the valve is fully closed.

Reasons for Adjusting the Mixture

Correct leaning of the engine mixture will enable the engine to be operated at its most efficient in terms of fuel consumption. With the increased use of 100LL fuel, leaning is also important to reduce spark plug fouling.

The most efficient engine operation is obtained with a fuel/air ratio of about 1:15; that is, 1 part fuel to 15 parts air. In fact with the mixture set to full rich, the system is designed to give a slightly richer mixture than ideal, typically about 1:12. This slightly over-rich mixture reduces the possibility of pre-ignition or detonation, and aids cylinder cooling.

As altitude increases, the air density decreases. Above about 3,000 feet, the reduced air density can lead to an over-rich mixture. If the mixture becomes excessively rich, power will be lost, rough running may be evident and ultimately engine failure will occur due to a "rich-out." It is for this reason that the mixture control is provided to ensure the correct fuel/air ratio; typically it is used when cruising above 3,000 feet.

The flight manuals for some older aircraft recommend leaning only above 5,000 feet. However, with the increasing use of AVGAS 100LL, and the plug fouling problems sometimes associated with 100LL, most operators recommend leaning once above 3,000 feet.

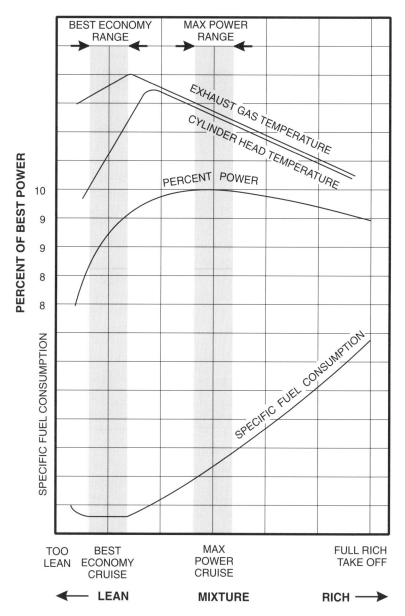

Use of the Mixture Control

For takeoff and climb the mixture should be fully rich; the only exception is operation from a high altitude airport when leaning may be necessary to ensure the availability of maximum power. On reaching a cruising altitude above about 3,000 feet the cruise power should be set, and then leaning can be carried out. (Note: Generally, leaning with over 75% power set is not recommended.) If climbing above about 5,000 feet, full throttle will be less than 75% power on a normally aspirated engine and so leaning may be permissible to maintain smooth running.

Assuming that there is no Exhaust Gas Temperature (EGT) gauge and no cylinder head temperature gauge, the primary instrument to watch when leaning is the RPM gauge (tachometer).

To lean the engine, the recommended power setting (RPM) is set with the throttle. Next, with a constant throttle setting, the mixture control is slowly moved back (leaned). If leaning is required the RPM will increase slowly, peak, and then decrease as the mixture is leaned; if leaning is continued the engine will ultimately run rough and lose power.

If the mixture is set to achieve peak RPM, the maximum power mixture has been achieved.

If the mixture is set to give a tachometer reading 25 to 50 RPM less than peak RPM on the "lean" side, the best economy mixture has been achieved. This setting is the one that many aircraft manufacturers recommend, and their performance claims are based on such a procedure.

Using a mixture that is too lean is a false economy, and will lead to serious engine damage sooner or later. Detonation (an uncontrolled explosive combustion of the mixture in the cylinder) is particularly dangerous, and can lead to an engine failure in a very short time. The use of a full rich mixture during full power operations is specifically to ensure engine cooling and guard against detonation.

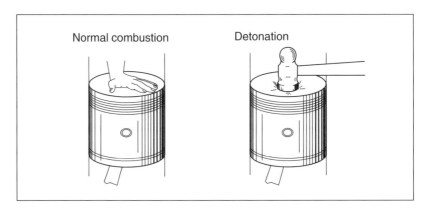

Normal combustion   Detonation

For any change in operating conditions (altitude, power setting) the mixture will need to be reset. It is particularly important that the mixture is set to full rich before increasing the power setting.

During a descent from a high altitude, the mixture will gradually become too lean if not enriched, leading to excessive cylinder temperatures, power loss and ultimately engine failure. Normally the mixture is set to full rich prior to landing, unless operating at a high elevation airfield.

Moving the mixture to the full lean position—ICO (idle cut-off)—closes the needle valve and so stops fuel supply to the main metering jet. This is the normal method for shutting down the engine and ensures that no un-burned fuel mixture is left in the engine.

Section 5
Expanded C152
Pre-Flight Checklist

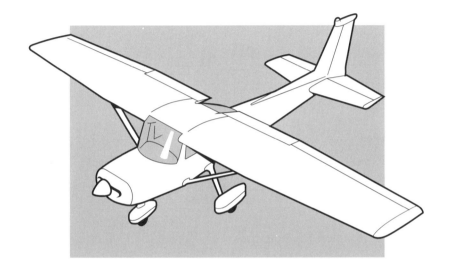

Approaching Aircraft

1. Check for and remove any tie-downs, external control locks, pitot cover and wheel chocks.

2. Look for any oil and fuel spillage from aircraft.

3. Remove any ice and frost from *all* surfaces.

4. Check for access to taxiways, obstructions, loose gravel, etc.

5. Look to see if aircraft is on a level surface. A sloping surface will effect the visual check of fuel quantity.

In Cabin

1. **Internal Control Locks and Covers** .... Remove, stow securely.

2. **Magneto Switch** .... Check OFF and key out.

3. **Parking Brake** ... Ensure parking brake is set by pushing on strut.

4. **Control Wheel Lock** .... Remove and stow.

5. **Master Switch** ...... On. Turn on Pitot heater, anti-collision beacon, landing lights and navigation lights. Leave cockpit and check—

6. **Pitot Heat** .... Check with fingers that pitot tube is warm (it may take a minute or so to warm up).

7. **Anti-Collision Beacon** .... Check operation of rotating tail light.

8. **Landing/Nav lights** .... Check. For navigation lights colors are: PORT (Left) – red; STARBOARD (Right) – green; REAR (Tail) – white

   Return to cockpit and turn off electrical services.

9. **Fuel Shut-off Valve** .... Check on; check quantity gauges.

10. **Flaps** .... Check flap area clear. Lower fully (30°).

11. **Master Switch** .... Off.

12. **Trim Wheel** .... Check position neutral using cockpit indicator.

13. **First Aid Kit** .... Check in position, secure.

14. **Fire Extinguisher** .... Check in position, secure and serviceable (gauge at top should be in green arc).

    Leave cockpit; watch your head on the lowered flaps!

Cessna 152 A Pilot's Guide

External
Begin at the rear of the wing. This should also be where you complete your checks.

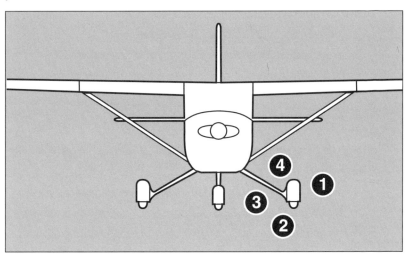

Port Landing Gear

1. **Tire** .... Check for tread and general condition. Check for correct inflation. Check alignment of creep marks.

2. **Hydraulic Lines** .... Check for leaks (red fluid).

3. **Disc Brake** .... Should be shiny, not rusty or pitted.

4. **Strut and Fairing** .... Check condition, especially fiberglass fairing. Look for mud or stone damage on wing and flap surface above or behind landing gear.

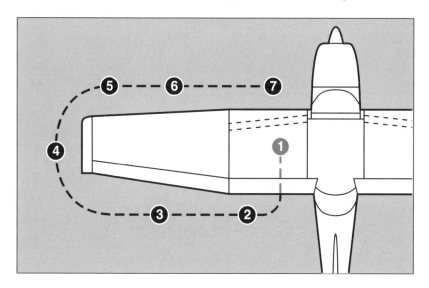

Port Wing

1. **Wing Strut** .... Check condition and security of strut and fairing.

2. **Flap** .... Check upper and lower surface condition. Particularly check lower surface for mud or stone damage from wheels. Check linkages and runners secure and greased

3. **Aileron** .... Check upper and lower surface condition. Linkages and hinges secure. With fingers inside hinge line (hold the aileron still with other hand), check balance weight is secure (lower inside edge). Check full and free movement—*do not use force*.

4. **Wing Tip** .... Check condition, security, navigation lights unbroken. (This area is particularly vulnerable to hangar damage)

5. **Lower Wing Surface** .... Check surface condition.

6. **Wing Leading Edge** .... Check for dents along entire length. Check stall warning horn. Check pitot tube perforations unblocked— *do not blow into pitot tube*. Check fuel tank vent unblocked. Check leading edge landing light.

7. **Fuel Tank** .... Check fuel quantity visually. Resecure cap. While at fuel cap check upper wing surface condition. Take fuel drain sample from under tank if necessary—check for correct color, water bubbles or sediment. Check that the drain is not leaking.

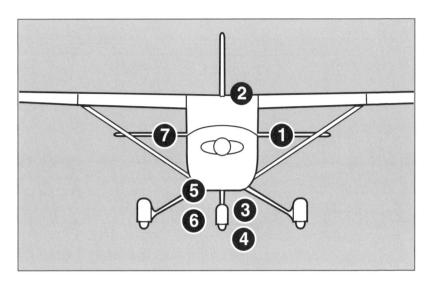

Front Fuselage and Engine

1. **Port Cowling** .... Check general condition and security. Check static vent clear—*do not blow into vent*.

2. **Windscreen** .... Should be clean and insect free.

3. **Nose Strut** .... Check oleo extension. Check linkage, nuts and split pins secure. No leakage from shimmy damper or oleo.

4. **Nose Wheel** .... Check for tread and general condition. Check for correct inflation. Check alignment of creep marks.

5. **Front Cowling** .... Check condition and security. Intakes clear, landing lights unbroken.

6. **Propeller** .... Look for cracks or chips, especially along the leading edge. Check spinner is secure and condition good. *Do not move or swing propeller.*

7. **Starboard Cowling** .... Open access flap, check oil level. Do *not* overtighten dipstick on resecuring. Operate fuel strainer, if applicable, into a fuel tester. Check fuel strainer is closed and not leaking. Check access flap is properly closed, cowling secure and good condition.

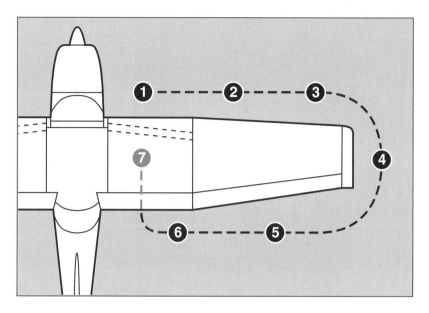

Starboard Wing

1. **Fuel Tank** .... Check fuel quantity visually. Resecure cap. Check upper wing surface. Take fuel drain sample if necessary from under wing. Check that the drain is not leaking.

2. **Wing Leading Edge** .... Check for dents along entire length.

3. **Lower Wing Surface** .... Check surface condition.

4. **Wing Tip** .... Check condition, security, navigation lights unbroken.

5. **Aileron** .... Check upper and lower surface condition. Linkages and hinges secure, balance weight (lower inside edge) secure. Remember to watch for aileron movement while checking inside hinge line. Check full and free movement gently—*do not use force.*

6. **Flap** .... Check upper and lower surface condition especially above and behind landing gear. Check linkage and tracks are secure and greased.

7. **Wing Strut** .... Check condition and security of strut and fairings.

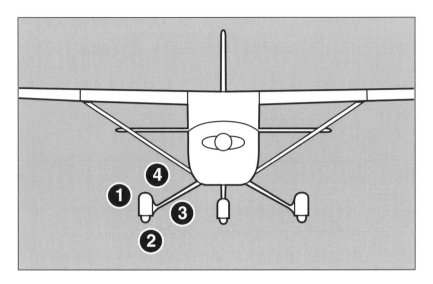

Starboard Landing Gear

1. **Tire** .... Check for tread and general condition. Check for correct inflation. Check alignment of creep marks.

2. **Hydraulic Lines** .... Check for leaks (red fluid).

3. **Disc Brake** .... Should be shiny, not rusty or pitted.

4. **Strut and Fairing** .... Check condition especially fiberglass fairing. Look for mud or stone damage on wing and flap surface near landing gear.

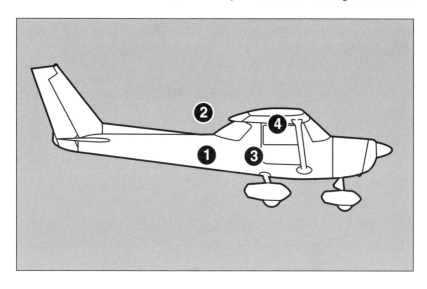

Starboard Fuselage

1. **Skin**.. Check general surface condition upper and lower, check for wrinkles, dents or punctures.

2. **Radio Antennas** .... Check secure.

3. **Cockpit Door** .... Check latches and hinges secure.

4. **Windows** .... Check clean.

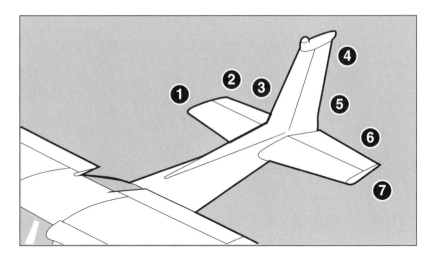

Tail Unit

1. **Starboard Horizontal Stabilizer** .... Check upper and lower surface condition, check security.

2. **Starboard Elevator** .... Check upper and lower surface condition. Check linkages and gently check full and free movement—*do not use force*.

3. **Trim Tab** .... Check condition, linkage and correct movement in relation to elevator.

4. **Tail Fin** .... Check condition, fairings, antennas and rotating beacon.

5. **Rudder** .... Check condition, navigation light, nuts and split pins, full and free movement—*do not use force*. Check tail tie-down point.

6. **Port Elevator** .... Check condition, linkage. Gently check full and free movement—*do not use force*.

7. **Port Horizontal Stabilizer** .... Check condition and security.

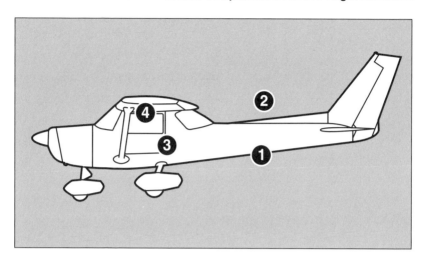

Port Fuselage

1. **Skin** .... Check general surface condition, upper and lower. Look for any wrinkles, dents or punctures.

2. **Radio Antennas** .... Check secure.

3. **Cockpit Door** .... Check latches and hinges.

4. **Windows** .... Check clean.

IMPORTANT

Remember: Full reference must be made to airplane flight manual,
Pilot's Operating Handbook, flight school syllabus, etc.,
for all normal and emergency procedures.

If in doubt—ask

Section 6
C152 Loading
and Performance

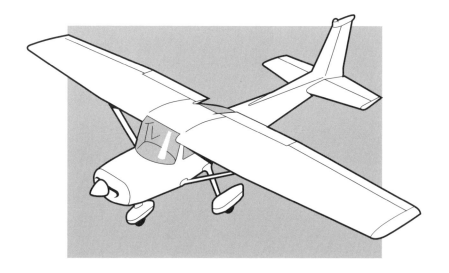

Loading

Aircraft loading can be divided into two areas: the aircraft weight, and the center of gravity (CG) position.

The aircraft must be loaded so that its weight is below the certified maximum takeoff weight—1,670 lbs. The flight manual may also list a "ramp weight," which is the maximum permissible weight for taxiing prior to takeoff. The difference between this and the maximum takeoff weight allows for the fuel used in starting, taxiing and power checks. The weight limit is set primarily as a function of the lifting capability of the aircraft, which is largely determined by the wing design and engine power of the aircraft. Operating the aircraft when it is over weight will adversely effect the aircraft handling and performance, such as:

Increased takeoff speed and slower acceleration

Increased runway length required for takeoff

Reduced rate of climb

Reduced maximum altitude capability

Reduced range and endurance

Reduction in maneuverability and controllability

Increased stall speed

Increased approach and landing speed

Increased runway length required for landing

The aircraft must also be loaded to ensure that its center of gravity (CG) is within set limits, normally defined as a forward and aft limit; for this aircraft the datum is the lower forward face of the firewall. The forward limit is determined by the amount of elevator control available at landing speed, the aft limit is determined by the stability and controllability of the aircraft while maneuvering. Attempted flight with the CG position outside the set limits (either forward or aft) will lead to control difficulties and quite possibly loss of control of the aircraft.

When loading the aircraft, it is standard practice to calculate the weight and CG position of the aircraft at the same time, commonly known as the weight and balance calculation. Before going further it must be emphasized that the following examples are provided for illustrative purposes only. Each *individual* aircraft has an *individual* weight and balance record that is valid only for that aircraft, and is dependent among other things on the equipment installed in the aircraft. If the aircraft has any major modification, repair, or new equipment fitted, a new weight and balance record will be produced. Therefore, for any loading or performance calculations, you must use the documents for the specific aircraft you will be using.

As well as setting out limits, the aircraft documents will also give arms for each item of loading. The arm is a distance from the aircraft datum to the item. The weight multiplied by its arm gives its moment. Thus, a set weight will have a greater moment the further away from the datum it is.

The operating weight of the aircraft can be split into two categories:

EMPTY WEIGHT—the weight of the aircraft, including unusable fuel (and normally full oil). The weight and CG position of the aircraft in this condition will be noted in the weight and balance record.

USEFUL LOAD—weight of a pilot, passenger, usable fuel and baggage. Again, the weight and balance record will give an arm for each of these loads.

Each individual aircraft has an individual weight and balance record, valid only for that aircraft. The weight and balance record will state arms for each item of loading.

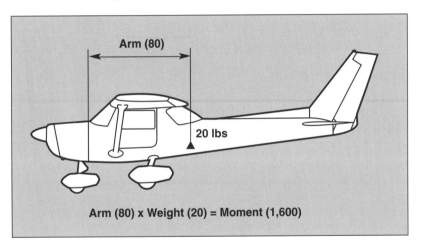

Arm (80) x Weight (20) = Moment (1,600)

Weight and Center of Gravity Record

Produced by:

Cessna Aircraft Company

Aircraft Type:

Cessna 152

Nationality and Registration Marks:

N-12345

Constructor's Serial Number:

78A0336

Maximum Permissible Weight:

1,675 lbs

Maximum Landing Weight:

1,670 lbs

Center of Gravity Limits:

Refer to Flight Manual Rep No. FAA 2126

All arms are distances in inches either fore or aft of datum.

Part "A" Basic Weight

The basic weight of this aircraft as calculated from Planeweighs Limited Report No. 1034 weighed on 08.07.88. at Manchester Airport is: **1,150 lbs**

The center of gravity of aircraft in the same condition (aft of the datum) is: **29.57 inches**

The total Moment about the datum in this condition in lb inches is: **34.0 lbs-in/1,000**

The DATUM referred to is defined in the Flight Manual, which is **66.25 inches** forward of wing leading edge.

The basic weight includes the weight of 9 lbs unusable fuel and 11.25 lbs of oil and the weight of items indicated in Appendix 1 which comprises the list of basic equipment carried.

Mathematical Weight and Balance Calculation

With this method of calculation the weights of each item are listed together with their arm. Addition of all the weights is the first step, to ensure that the resulting figure is within the maximum permitted. Assuming this is the case the balance can then be calculated. For each item (except the basic weight where the calculation is already done on the weight and balance record) the weight is multiplied by the arm, to give the moment. Normally the arm is aft of the datum, to give a positive figure. If the arm quoted is forward of the datum, the arm and resulting moment will be negative (although obviously the weight is *not* deducted from the weight calculation). All the moments are then added together, to give the total moment, and this figure is then divided by the total weight. The resulting figure will be the position of the CG, which can be checked to ensure it is within the set limits. Alternatively, the weight and CG position can be plotted on the center of gravity limits graph in the flight manual. If the plotted position is within the "envelope," the weight and CG position are within limits.

Example:

EMPTY WEIGHT: Aircraft N-1234
                       From the weight and balance record for N-1234
                       weight is 1,150.7 lbs.

USEFUL LOAD: Pilot 160 lbs
                       Passenger 150 lbs
                       Baggage (Area 1) 30 lbs
                       Full Usable Fuel (24.5 US gal) 147 lbs

Using the known weight of each item, and the arm given in the weight and balance record, a table can be used to calculate the moment for each item (moment = weight x arm).

ITEM	WEIGHT (lbs)	ARM (in)	MOMENT (lb-in)
EMPTY WEIGHT—from the weight and balance record for N-1234 the weight, arm and moment are all listed.			
N-1234	1,150.7	29.7	34,176
USEFUL LOAD			
Pilot	160	39.0	6,240
Passenger	150	39.0	5,850
Baggage (area 1)	30	64.0	1,920
Full (usable) fuel	147	40.0	5,880
TOTAL WEIGHT	1,637.7	TOTAL MOMENT	54,066

You can see that the weight at 1,637.7 lbs is below the maximum permitted of 1,670 lbs. To find the center of gravity position, the total moment is divided by total weight:

$$\frac{54,066}{1,637.7} = 33.01 \text{ inches aft of datum}$$

The weight and center of gravity position can be plotted on the center of gravity limits graph. It shows that the loading is within limits.

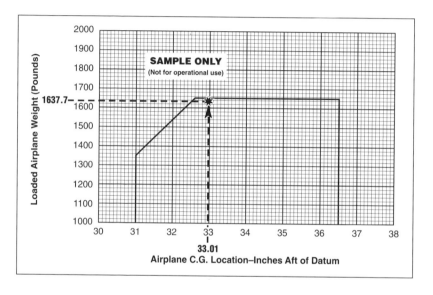

Use of the Loading Graph

The mathematical calculation of loading can be tedious, especially without a calculator!

The loading graph allows a quicker loading calculation by automatically multiplying the weight of each item by the relevant arm. The downside is a slightly less accurate result.

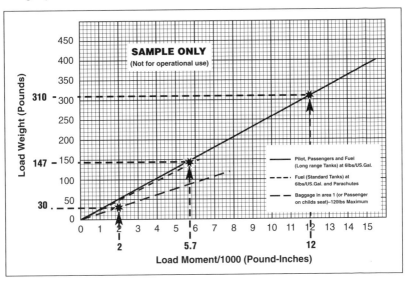

Using the figures from the previous example, we can use the loading graph to create a simplified table:

ITEM	WEIGHT (lbs)	MOMENT/1,000 (lb-in)
Basic A/C	1,150.7	34.1
Pilot/Passenger	310	12
Baggage (Area 1)	30	2
Usable fuel	147	5.7
TOTAL WEIGHT 1,637.7		53.8

As you can see the total moment is slightly different to that when using the mathematical calculation.

Again moment (/1,000) can be divided by weight (/1,000) to give the center of gravity position

$$\frac{53.8}{1.6377} = 32.85 \text{ inches aft of datum}$$

The weight and center of gravity position is plotted on the center of gravity limits envelope to check it is within limits.

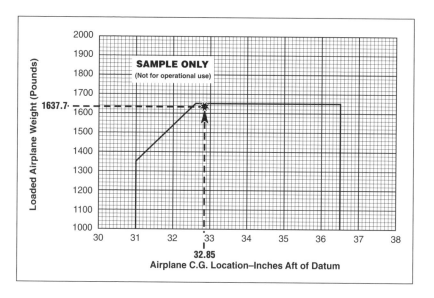

The slightly different answer is due to the less accurate nature of the loading graph. If in any doubt, a mathematical calculation will give an exact answer.

One further way to reduce the arithmetic in the loading calculation is to plot the TOTAL weight against the TOTAL moment on the center of gravity moment envelope graph. The figures can come from either the mathematical or loading graph method of calculation, there is no need to divide total moment by total weight.

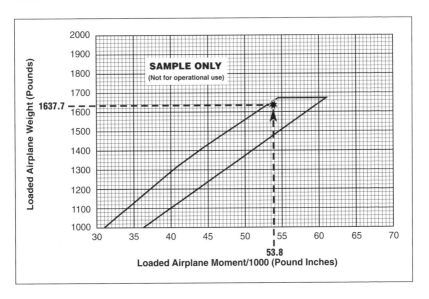

Always be clear which graph you are using and why. The center of gravity limits graph can only be used if you have divided moment by weight to find the center of gravity position.

Differing flight manuals and differing weight and balance records may use different units (i.e., meters or inches, kg or lbs, etc.). Always know which units you are working in, they may not be the ones you thought!

A WORD OF WARNING. As well as the safety aspect, operating the aircraft outside its weight and balance envelope has far-reaching legal and financial implications. Almost the first thing an accident investigator will check after an accident is the loading of the aircraft. If the loading is outside limits the pilot is violating the Federal Aviation Regulations. In addition, both the aircraft insurance company and the your personal insurance company will be unsympathetic when they know that the conditions of the Airworthiness Certificate (i.e., the flight manual limitations) were not complied with. As the pilot-in-command the responsibility is yours alone. The fact that the aircraft has two seats does not necessarily mean that the aircraft can be flown with both seats occupied, maximum baggage and full fuel load. This is particularly true if the aircraft is fitted with the long range fuel tanks option.

C152 Center of Gravity Limits

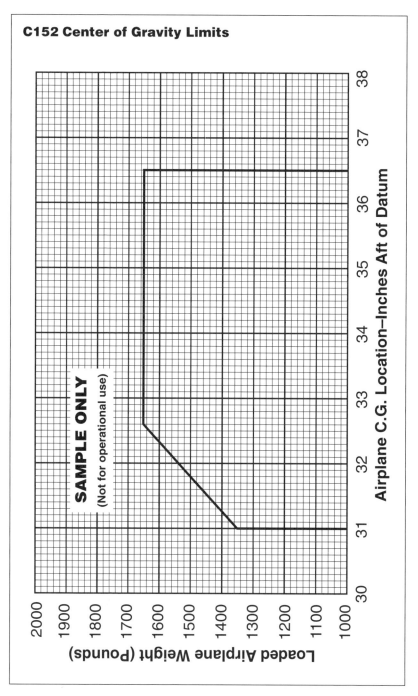

SAMPLE ONLY
(Not for operational use)

Loaded Airplane Weight (Pounds)

Airplane C.G. Location–Inches Aft of Datum

C152 Loading Graph

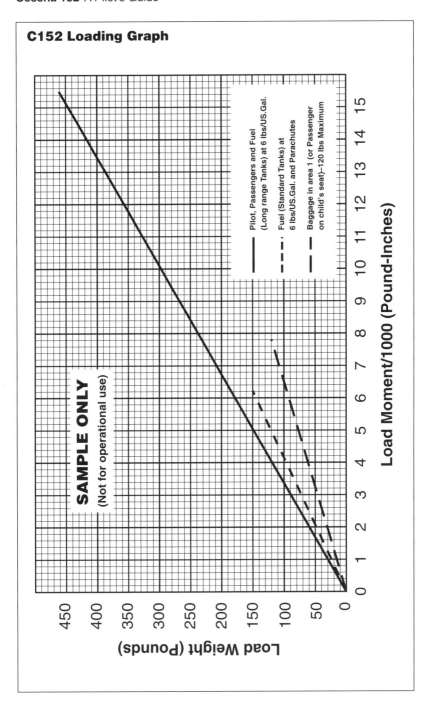

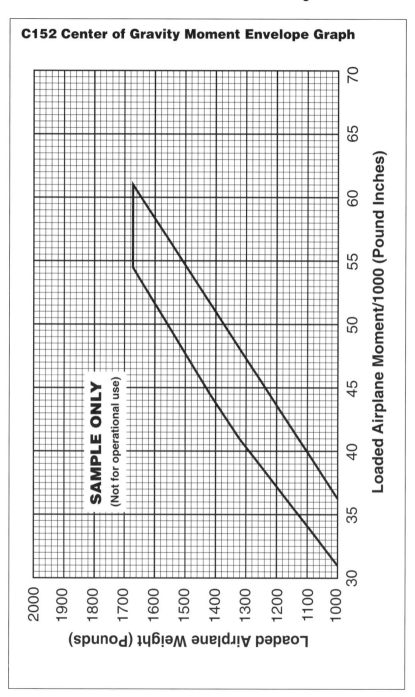

C152 Center of Gravity Moment Envelope Graph

SAMPLE ONLY
(Not for operational use)

Loaded Airplane Weight (Pounds)

Loaded Airplane Moment/1000 (Pound Inches)

Performance

The aircraft's flight manual contains a section of tables and graphs to allow the pilot to calculate the expected performance of the aircraft for different flight phases. Undoubtedly the most commonly used tables are those for takeoff and landing performance and those are the ones we will concentrate on here; however, the same principles can be used on the other tables. Two things to remember: first, the manual performance is obtained by using the recommended techniques—to get table results follow table procedures. Second, you can safely assume that the flight manual results have been obtained by placing a brand new aircraft in the hands of an experienced test pilot flying under favorable conditions. To make allowances for a less than new aircraft, being flown by an average mortal in real conditions it is wise to "factor" any results you get. As with loading calculations the pilot must use the tables and data from the documents for the individual aircraft being used. The tables and diagrams used in this section are for illustrative purposes only, and not for operational use.

In Section 7, conversion factors between feet and meters are listed, together with recommended factors for variations not necessarily covered by the flight manual tables.

C152 Takeoff and Landing Performance Tables

The takeoff and landing distance tables in the flight manual make several assumptions (e.g., paved level dry runway, use of flight manual technique, etc.).

Depending on the model year and country of manufacture, the table distances may be given in feet or meters. In addition the temperature may be in °C or °F, speeds in knots or kph, weight in lbs or kg, or any combination of these! This can be a recipe for confusion, so check the flight manual carefully to be sure what units you are using. Always apply a common sense check—if the results you are getting look more appropriate to an ultralight (or a 747) there may be a mistake; if in doubt—check.

The tables use the term "Pressure Altitude." This is the altitude of the runway assuming standard pressure setting (i.e., 29.92" Hg). If it is anything different you will need to adjust the actual altitude to get the pressure altitude. In the aircraft this can be done by simply setting the altimeter to 29.92" Hg and taking the indicated altitude. Without an altimeter handy adjust the actual altitude by 1,000 feet for each inch above or below 29.92" (10 feet for each .01").

The headwind or tailwind component is calculated from the wind speed and angle of wind direction to the runway, (e.g., a 10 knot wind directly down the runway gives a headwind component of 10 knots; a 10 knot wind at 90° gives a headwind component of zero). There is a graph in Section 7 for calculation of head/tailwind component and crosswind component.

The takeoff and landing distance tables will contain a reminder to check the flight manual recommended technique. To get the flight manual results you must use the flight manual technique.

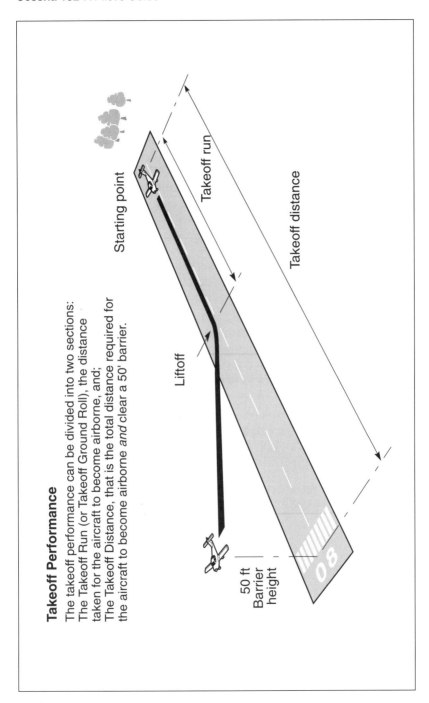

Takeoff Performance

The takeoff performance can be divided into two sections:
The Takeoff Run (or Takeoff Ground Roll), the distance taken for the aircraft to become airborne, and;
The Takeoff Distance, that is the total distance required for the aircraft to become airborne *and* clear a 50' barrier.

Starting point

Takeoff run

Takeoff distance

Liftoff

50 ft
Barrier
height

08

Takeoff Distance Calculation Example

Outside Air Temperature +15°C
Pressure Altitude 798 feet
Takeoff weight 1,670 lbs
Headwind Component 5 knots
Level dry short grass runway

As you can see, the temperature and pressure altitude figures do not exactly match the parameters of the table. The quickest and easiest way around this is to round UP the temperature and pressure altitude to the nearest parameter shown on the table, so use a pressure altitude of 1,000 feet and a temperature of +20°C. Using these figures gives a takeoff distance of 1,530 feet.

WEIGHT LBS.	TAKEOFF SPEED		PRESS ALT FT	0°C		10°C		20°C	
	LIFT OFF	AT 50 FT		GROUND ROLL FT	TOTAL FT TO CLEAR 50 FT. OBS.	GROUND ROLL FT	TOTAL FT TO CLEAR 50 FT. OBS.	GROUND ROLL FT	TOTAL FT TO CLEAR 50 FT. OBS.
1670	50	54	S.L.	640	1190	695	1290	755	1390
	KIAS	KIAS	1000	705	1310	765	1420	825	1530
			2000	775	1445	840	1565	910	1690
			3000	855	1600	925	1730	1000	1870

The headwind component of 5 knots is factored in accordance with the notes to the table—i.e., decrease takeoff distance by 10% for each 9 knots headwind; thus

$$\frac{5 \text{ knots}}{9 \text{ knots}} \text{ x } 10\% = 5.5\% \text{ (decrease in takeoff distance)}$$

When this reduction is applied to the figure of 1,530 feet, the new takeoff distance is 1,446 feet.

Now the takeoff distance must be factored for the effect of the short dry grass surface. Applying the correction given in the flight manual can be unnecessarily complicated; a better idea is to use the FAA recommended factor for a short dry grass surface—that is, 1.2 x takeoff distance (see page 7-3); thus

1,446' x 1.2 = 1,735'.

If you wish to mathematically calculate the exact figures based on proportioning the differences between the takeoff distances at different parameters, the whole process will take quite some time. Doing such a calculation based on the given conditions, still allowing a factor of 1.2 for

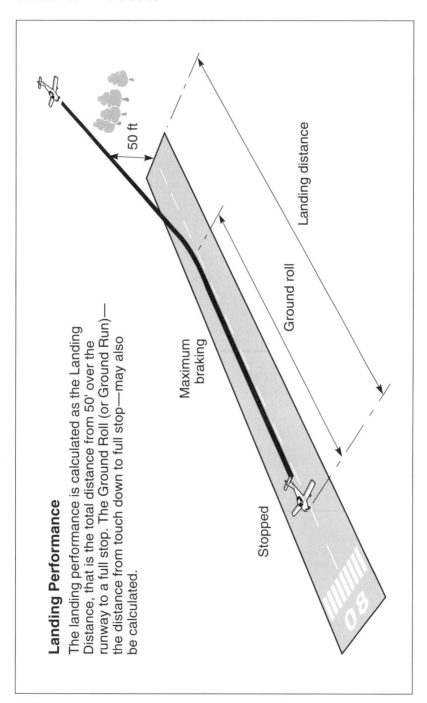

Landing Performance

The landing performance is calculated as the Landing Distance, that is the total distance from 50' over the runway to a full stop. The Ground Roll (or Ground Run)—the distance from touch down to full stop—may also be calculated.

50 ft

Landing distance

Ground roll

Maximum braking

Stopped

08

the short dry grass surface, gives an end result of 1,641 feet. Strictly speaking this answer is more accurate (and far more tedious to calculate!), but maybe it is better to regard the difference as a little extra safety margin for less than perfect pilots flying less than perfect aircraft in less than perfect conditions.

Landing Distance Calculation Example

Outside Air Temperature +10°C
Pressure Altitude 1690 feet
Landing Weight 1,670 lbs.
Headwind Component 11 knots
Dry level paved runway, with a 2% downslope.

WEIGHT LBS.	SPEED AT 50 FT	PRESS ALT FT	0°C		10°C		20°C	
			GROUND ROLL FT	TOTAL FT TO CLEAR 50 FT. OBS.	GROUND ROLL FT	TOTAL FT TO CLEAR 50 FT. OBS.	GROUND ROLL FT	TOTAL FT TO CLEAR 50 FT. OBS.
1670	54	S.L.	450	1160	465	1185	485	1215
	KIAS	1000	465	1185	485	1215	500	1240
		2000	485	1215	500	1240	520	1270
		3000	500	1240	520	1275	540	1305

First, the pressure altitude is rounded *up* to the nearest table parameter (2,000 feet). Against 2,000 feet and +10°C, a landing distance of 1,240 feet is read off. This figure is now factored to allow for the headwind component. Using the given factor on the table (i.e., decrease landing distance by 10% for each 9 knots headwind):

$$\frac{11 \text{ knots}}{9 \text{ knots}} \times 10\% = 12\% \text{ decrease in landing distance.}$$

So the landing distance is 1,240' − 12% (i.e., 1,240 x 0.88) = 1,091'.

From Section 7 (page 7-4), the FAA recommended factor for a 2% downhill slope is a 10% increase in landing distance. Therefore:

$$1,091' \times 1.1 = 1,200'$$

C152 Takeoff Distances – Short Field

WEIGHT LBS.	TAKEOFF SPEED LIFT OFF	TAKEOFF SPEED AT 50 FT	PRESS ALT FT	0°C/32°F GROUND ROLL FT	0°C/32°F TOTAL FT TO CLEAR 50 FT. OBS.	10°C/50°F GROUND ROLL FT	10°C/50°F TOTAL FT TO CLEAR 50 FT. OBS.	20°C/68°F GROUND ROLL FT	20°C/68°F TOTAL FT TO CLEAR 50 FT. OBS.	30°C/86°F GROUND ROLL FT	30°C/86°F TOTAL FT TO CLEAR 50 FT. OBS.	40°C/100°F GROUND ROLL FT	40°C/100°F TOTAL FT TO CLEAR 50 FT. OBS.
1670	50 KIAS	54 KIAS	S.L.	640	1190	695	1290	755	1390	810	1495	875	1605
			1000	705	1310	765	1420	825	1530	890	1645	960	1770
			2000	775	1445	840	1565	910	1690	980	1820	1055	1960
			3000	855	1600	925	1730	1000	1870	1080	2020	1135	2185
			4000	940	1775	1020	1920	1100	2080	1190	2250	1285	2440
			5000	1040	1970	1125	2140	1215	2320	1315	2525	1420	2750
			6000	1145	2200	1245	2395	1345	2610	1455	2855	1570	3125
			7000	1270	2470	1375	2705	1490	2960	1615	3255	1745	3590
			8000	1405	2800	1525	3080	1655	3395	1795	3765	1940	4195

C152 Landing Distances – Short Field

WEIGHT LBS.	SPEED AT 50 FT	PRESS ALT FT	0°C/32°F		10°C/50°F		20°C/68°F		30°C/86°F		40°C/100°F	
			GROUND ROLL FT	TOTAL FT TO CLEAR 50 FT. OBS.	GROUND ROLL FT	TOTAL FT TO CLEAR 50 FT. OBS.	GROUND ROLL FT	TOTAL FT TO CLEAR 50 FT. OBS.	GROUND ROLL FT	TOTAL FT TO CLEAR 50 FT. OBS.	GROUND ROLL FT	TOTAL FT TO CLEAR 50 FT. OBS.
1670	54 KIAS	S.L.	450	1160	465	1185	485	1215	500	1240	515	1265
		1000	465	1185	485	1215	500	1240	520	1270	535	1295
		2000	485	1215	500	1240	520	1270	535	1300	555	1330
		3000	500	1240	520	1275	540	1305	560	1335	575	1360
		4000	520	1275	540	1305	560	1335	580	1370	600	1400
		5000	540	1305	560	1335	580	1370	600	1400	620	1435
		6000	560	1340	590	1370	605	1410	625	1440	645	1475
		7000	585	1375	605	1410	625	1440	650	1480	670	1515
		8000	605	1410	630	1450	650	1480	675	1520	695	1555

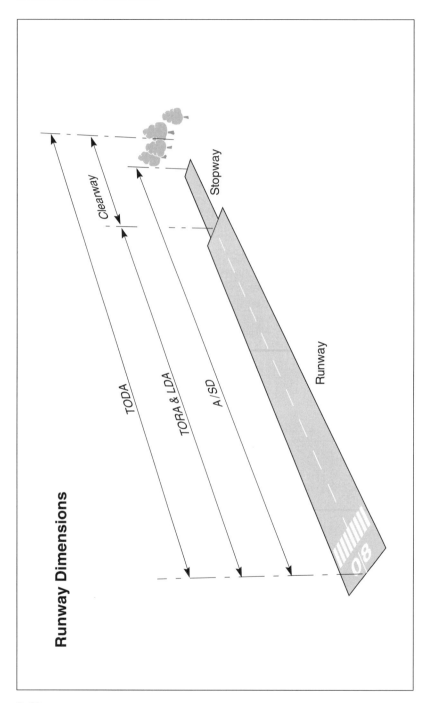

Runway Dimensions

En Route Performance

The flight manual has tables to calculate cruise performance. It is wise to factor the cruise performance figures by at least 10% (i.e., increase fuel consumption by 10%), and remember the figures are based on the use of the flight manual recommended mixture leaning procedure. If you do not use this recommended procedure you are unlikely to achieve the table figures.

It is also necessary to allow an adequate fuel reserve—30 minutes day, 45 minutes night (this may be allowed for in the table figures—check to be sure). The infinite number of variables that can effect any flight (e.g., stronger than forecast headwinds, change of routing, higher than expected fuel consumption, delay at holding point prior to departure, etc.) make it foolhardy to attempt to fly to the very limit of calculated range or endurance.

Runway Dimensions

Having calculated the distances the aircraft requires for takeoff or landing, the runway dimensions must be checked to ensure that the aircraft can be safely operated on the runway in question. The figures given in the Airport/ Facility Directory or airfield guide can be defined in a number of ways.

The Takeoff Run Available (TORA)

The TORA is the length of the runway available for the takeoff ground run of the aircraft. This is usually the physical length of the runway.

The Accelerate/Stop Distance (A/SD)

The A/SD is the length of the TORA plus the length of any stopway. A stopway is an area at the end of the TORA prepared for an aircraft to stop on in the event of an abandoned takeoff.

The Takeoff Distance Available (TODA)

The TODA is the TORA plus the length of any clearway. A clearway is an area over which an aircraft may make its initial climb (to 50 feet in this instance).

The Landing Distance Available (LDA)

The LDA is the length of the runway available for the ground run of an aircraft landing. In all cases the landing distance required should never be greater than the landing distance available.

CRUISE PERFORMANCE

CESSNA MODEL 152

CONDITIONS : 1,670 Pounds Recommended Lean Mixture (See Section, 4, Cruise)

NOTE: Cruise speeds are shown for an airplane equipped with speed fairings which increase the speeds by approximately two knots.

PRESSURE ALTITUDE FT	RPM	20°C BELOW STANDARD TEMP			STANDARD TEMP			20°C ABOVE STANDARD TEMP		
		% BHP	KTAS	GPH	% BHP	KTAS	GPH	% BHP	KTAS	GPH
2000	2400	—	—	—	75	101	6.1	70	101	5.7
	2300	71	97	5.7	66	96	5.4	63	95	5.1
	2200	62	92	5.1	59	91	4.8	56	90	4.6
	2100	55	87	4.5	53	86	4.3	51	85	4.2
	2000	49	81	4.1	47	80	3.9	46	79	3.8
4000	2450	—	—	—	75	103	6.1	70	102	5.7
	2400	76	102	6.1	71	101	5.7	67	100	5.4
	2300	67	96	5.4	63	95	5.1	60	95	4.9
	2200	60	91	4.8	56	90	4.6	54	89	4.4
	2100	53	86	4.4	51	85	4.2	49	84	4.0
	2000	48	81	3.9	46	80	3.8	45	78	3.7
6000	2500	—	—	—	75	105	6.1	71	104	5.7
	2400	72	101	5.8	67	100	5.4	64	99	5.2
	2300	64	96	5.2	60	95	4.9	57	94	4.7
	2200	57	90	4.6	54	89	4.4	52	88	4.3
	2100	51	85	4.2	49	84	4.0	48	83	3.9
	2000	46	80	3.8	45	79	3.7	44	77	3.6
8000	2550	—	—	—	75	107	6.1	71	106	5.7
	2500	76	105	6.2	71	104	5.8	67	103	5.4
	2400	68	100	5.5	64	99	5.2	61	98	4.9
	2300	61	95	5.0	58	94	4.7	55	93	4.5
	2200	55	90	4.5	52	89	4.3	51	87	4.2
	2100	49	84	4.1	48	83	3.9	46	82	3.8
10,000	2500	72	105	5.8	68	103	5.5	64	103	5.2
	2400	65	99	5.3	61	98	5.0	58	97	4.8
	2300	58	94	4.7	56	93	4.5	53	92	4.4
	2200	53	89	4.3	51	88	4.2	49	86	4.0
	2100	48	83	4.0	46	82	3.9	45	81	3.8
12,000	2450	65	101	5.3	62	100	5.0	59	99	4.8
	2400	62	99	5.0	59	97	4.8	56	96	4.6
	2300	56	93	4.6	54	92	4.4	52	91	4.3
	2200	51	88	4.2	49	87	4.1	48	85	4.0
	2100	47	82	3.9	45	81	3.8	44	79	3.7

Section 7
Conversions

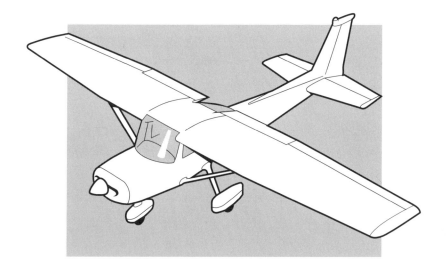

Takeoff Distance Factors

The following factors will allow the pilot to make allowance for variations that may affect takeoff performance. Although some of these factors are covered in the C152 performance tables, the table is produced in its entirety for completeness:

VARIATION	INCREASE IN TAKEOFF DISTANCE (to 50')	FACTOR
10% increase in aircraft weight	20%	1.2
Increase of 1,000' in runway altitude	10%	1.1
Increase in temperature of 10°C	10%	1.1
Dry Grass		
—Short (under 5 inches)	20%	1.2
—Long (5 – 10 inches)	25%	1.25
Wet Grass		
—Short	25%	1.25
—Long	30%	1.3
2% uphill slope	10%	1.1
Tailwind component of 10% of lift-off speed	20%	1.2
Soft ground or snow *	at least 25%	at least 1.25

* snow and other runway contamination are covered on page 7-5.

Landing Distance Factors

The following factors will allow the pilot to make allowance for variations that may affect landing performance. Although some of these factors are covered in the C152 performance tables, the table is produced in its entirety for completeness:

VARIATION	INCREASE IN LANDING DISTANCE (from 50')	FACTOR
10% increase in aircraft weight	10%	1.1
Increase of 1,000' in runway altitude	5%	1.05
Increase in temperature of 10°C	5%	1.05
Dry Grass		
—Short (under 5 inches)	20%	1.2
—Long (5 – 10 inches)	30%	1.3
Wet Grass		
—Short	30%	1.30
—Long	40%	1.40
2% downhill slope	10%	1.1
Tailwind component of 10% of landing speed	20%	1.2
snow *	at least 25%	at least 1.25
* snow and other runway contamination are covered on page 7-5.		

Runway Contamination

A runway can be contaminated by water, snow or slush. If operation on such a runway cannot be avoided, additional allowance must be made for the problems such contamination may cause—i.e., additional drag, reduced braking performance (possible hydroplaning), and directional control problems.

It is generally recommended that takeoff should not be attempted if dry snow covers the runway to a depth of more than 2", or if water, slush or wet snow covers the runway to more than 1/2". In addition, a tailwind or crosswind component exceeding 10 knots, should not be accepted when operating on a slippery runway.

For takeoff distance required calculations, the other known conditions should be factored, and the accelerate/stop distance available on the runway should be at least 2.0 x the takeoff distance required (for a paved runway) or at least 2.66 x the takeoff distance required (for a grass runway).

Any water or slush can have a very adverse effect on landing performance, and the danger of hydroplaning (with negligible wheel braking and loss of directional control) is very real.

Use of the Wind Component Graph

This graph can be used to find the head/tail wind component and the crosswind component, given a particular wind velocity and runway direction.

EXAMPLE:

Runway 27

Surface wind 240°/15 knots

The angle between the runway direction (270°) and wind direction(240°) is 30°. Now on the graph locate a point on the 30° line, where it crosses the 15 knot arc. From this point take a horizontal line to give the headwind component (13 knots) and a vertical line to give the crosswind component (8 knots).

On the main graph overleaf the shaded area represents the maximum demonstrated crosswind component for this aircraft. If the wind point is within this shaded area, the maximum demonstrated crosswind component for this aircraft has been exceeded.

Note:
Runway direction will be degrees magnetic.
Check the wind direction given is also in degrees magnetic.

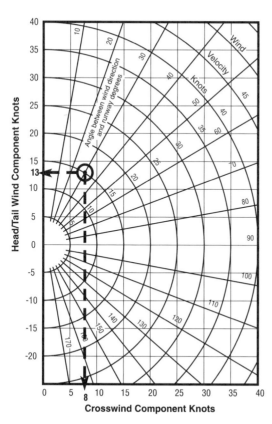

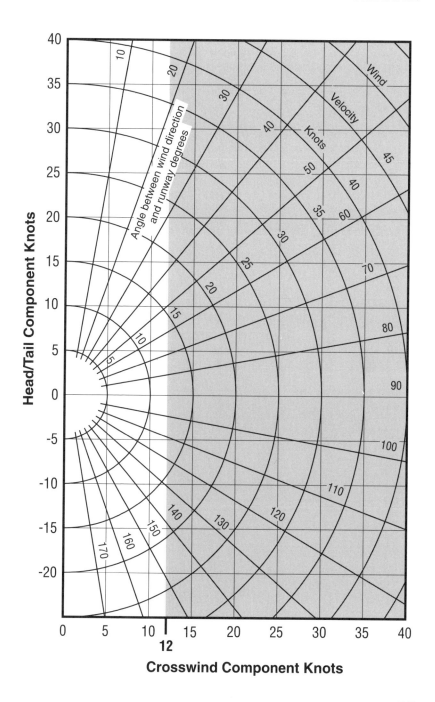

Crosswind Component Knots

Cessna 152 A Pilot's Guide

Temperature

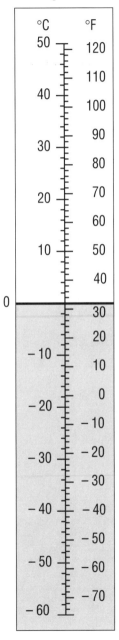

Distance – Meters/Feet

Meters	Feet		Feet	Meters
1	3.28		1	0.30
2	6.56		2	0.61
3	9.84		3	0.91
4	13.12		4	1.22
5	16.40		5	1.52
6	19.69		6	1.83
7	22.97		7	2.13
8	26.25		8	2.44
9	29.53		9	2.74
10	32.81		10	3.05
20	65.62		20	6.10
30	98.43		30	9.14
40	131.23		40	12.19
50	164.04		50	15.24
60	196.85		60	18.29
70	229.66		70	21.34
80	262.47		80	24.38
90	295.28		90	27.43
100	328.08		100	30.48
200	656.16		200	60.96
300	984.25		300	91.44
400	1,312.34		400	121.92
500	1,640.42		500	152.40
600	1,968.50		600	182.88
700	2,296.59		700	213.36
800	2,624.67		800	243.84
900	2,952.76		900	274.32
1,000	3,280.84		1,000	304.80
2,000	6,561.70		2,000	609.60
3,000	9,842.50		3,000	914.40
4,000	13,123.40		4,000	1,219.20
5,000	16,404.20		5,000	1,524.00
6,000	19,685.00		6,000	1,828.80
7,000	22,965.90		7,000	2,133.60
8,000	26,246.70		8,000	2,438.40
9,000	29,527.60		9,000	2,743.20
10,000	32,808.40		10,000	3,048.00

Conversion Factors:

Centimeters to Inches x .3937   Meters to Feet x 3.28084
Inches to Centimeters x 2.54   Feet to Meters x 0.3048

Distance – Nautical Miles / Statute Miles

NM	SM		SM	NM
1	1.15		1	.87
2	2.30		2	1.74
3	3.45		3	2.61
4	4.60		4	3.48
5	5.75		5	4.34
6	6.90		6	5.21
7	8.06		7	6.08
8	9.21		8	6.95
9	10.36		9	7.82
10	11.51		10	8.69
20	23.02		20	17.38
30	34.52		30	26.07
40	46.03		40	34.76
50	57.54		50	43.45
60	69.05		60	52.14
70	80.55		70	60.83
80	92.06		80	69.52
90	103.57		90	78.21
100	115.1		100	86.9
200	230.2		200	173.8
300	345.2		300	260.7
400	460.3		400	347.6
500	575.4		500	434.5
600	690.5		600	521.4
700	805.6		700	608.3
800	920.6		800	695.2
900	1035.7		900	782.1

Conversion Factors:

Statute Miles to Nautical Miles x 0.868976
Nautical Miles to Statute Miles x 1.15078

Volume (Fluid)

Liters	U.S. Gal.
1	0.26
2	0.53
3	0.79
4	1.06
5	1.32
6	1.59
7	1.85
8	2.11
9	2.38
10	2.64
20	5.28
30	7.93
40	10.57
50	13.21
60	15.85
70	18.49
80	21.14
90	23.78
100	26.42
200	52.84
300	79.26
400	105.68
500	132.10
600	158.52
700	184.94
800	211.36
900	237.78
1000	264.20

U.S. Gal.	Liters
1	3.79
2	7.57
3	11.36
4	15.14
5	18.93
6	22.71
7	26.50
8	30.28
9	34.07
10	37.85
20	75.71
30	113.56
40	151.41
50	189.27
60	227.12
70	264.97
80	302.82
90	340.68
100	378.54

Conversion Factors:
U.S. Gallons to Liters x 3.78541
Liters to U.S. Gallons x 0.264179

Cessna 152 A Pilot's Guide

C152 – Index

Cessna 152 A Pilot's Guide